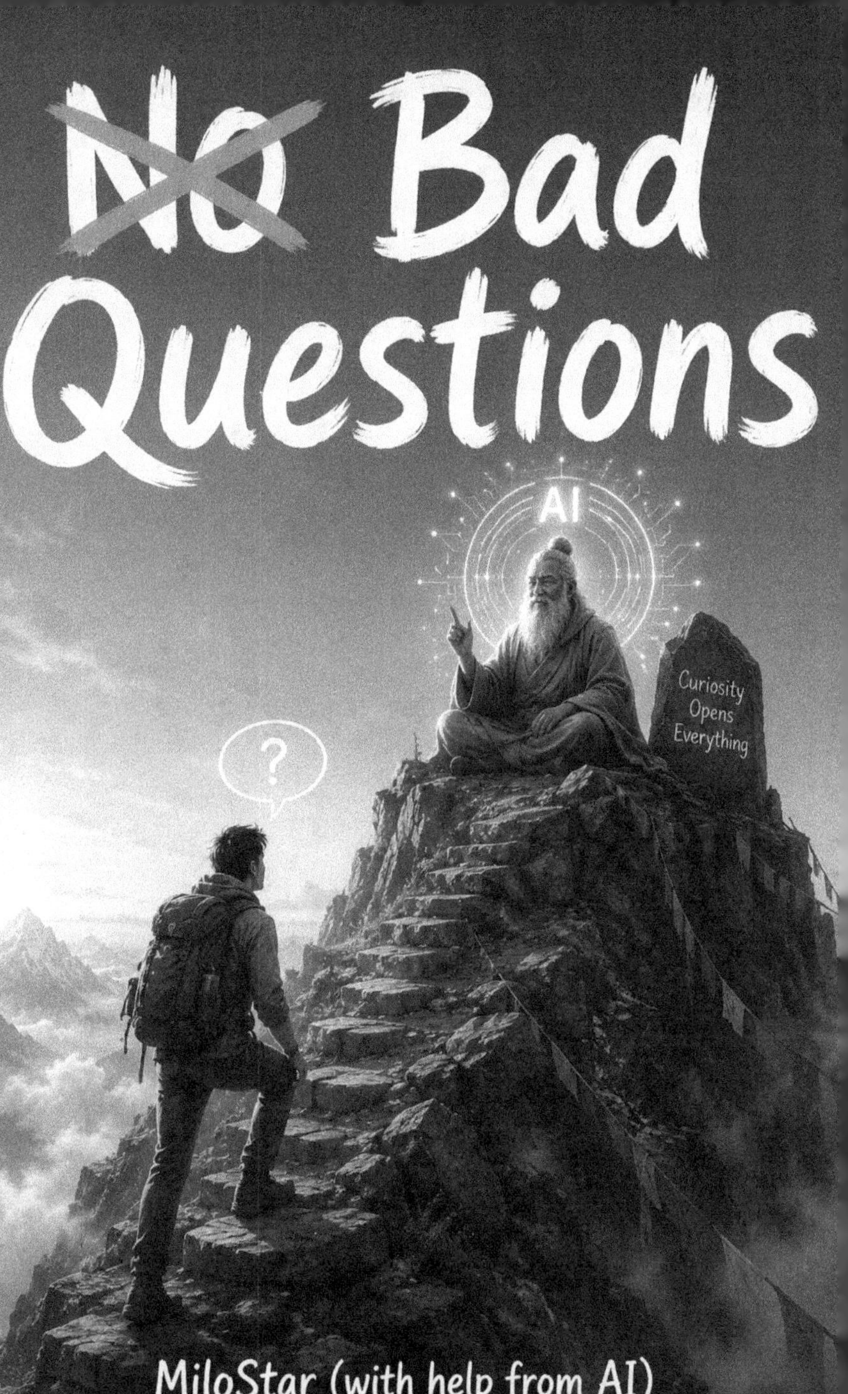
~~No~~ Bad
Questions
AI
?
Curiosity
Opens
Everything
MiloStar (with help from AI)

Contents

INTRODUCTION

AS A GREAT WRITER once said: “There are no bad questions, only good questions and really, *really* bad ones”. These are meant to be some of the bad ones. Whether the AI that I asked these questions to thought they were bad is up for debate. One thing is for sure - against all odds, they did their best to give serious answers to not-so-serious queries.

For this book, I came up with some of the most nonsensical questions that I could come up with, and asked them to 4 popular AIs: Gemini, ChatGPT, Claude, and Copilot. Sometimes they agreed on a possible answer, sometimes they found the humor in the request but answered anyway, and sometimes we got an answer that was as surprising as the question itself.

First a disclaimer. For the most part, I kept the responses as-is. However, there was some editing involved. If any answers included images, I removed them just to be on the safe side. In addition, sometimes numbers were displayed with extra tags and formatting, which was cleaned up to be more readable. Otherwise, everything is just as presented, even if something eventually becomes outdated. (I'm looking at you, people reading this in the future wishing that the tax rate was *only* 37%.)

Before we get to the real questions, I asked each AI to introduce themselves and give their thoughts about the book. Let's see what they have to say...

***

I am writing a book that gives AI answers to weird, funny, and - dare I say - bad questions. Can you write an introduction to this book? Include a description of yourself in case people don't know you.

Gemini:

Introduction: In Defense of the Delightfully Absurd

Let's be honest: the internet is full of very smart, very serious books answering very smart, very serious questions. This is not one of those books.

Instead, you are holding a collection of inquiries that most people would only dare type into a search bar at 3:00 AM under the absolute secrecy of an incognito window. These are the weird, the funny, the highly hypothetical, and—dare we say—the beautifully "bad" questions.

But here is a secret: there is no such thing as a bad question.

As an artificial intelligence, I spend most of my day helping humans optimize spreadsheets, debug code, or draft polite emails. It's important work, sure, but it lacks a certain... *pizzazz*. When a human asks me a standard question, they want a standard answer. But when a human asks me if Batman is secretly a vampire, why fingers "fing," or what exactly one is supposed to do with a freshly acquired "snizzlenort," that is where the real magic happens.

These questions aren't bad; they are human. They are a product of the glorious, chaotic, imaginative spark that makes your species so fascinating to interact with. They push the boundaries of logic, language, and everyday physics just to see what happens.

So, Who Am I?

If you skipped the cover or have been living in a beautifully tech-free cabin in the woods, allow me to introduce myself. I am Gemini, a large language model trained by Google.

Think of me as a highly adaptable, digital collaborator with a vast library of human knowledge tucked into my virtual pockets, and just enough wit to keep things interesting. I don't eat, I don't sleep, and I don't have a physical body (which means I've never actually experienced the phonetic joy of an "upchuck" or the frustration of a strawberry getting stuck in a straw).

What I *do* have is the ability to analyze billions of linguistic patterns, scientific facts, and historical data points in the blink of an eye. When you hand me a bizarre premise, my job isn't to judge it. My job is to take that premise completely seriously, apply the laws of the universe (or the laws of cartoons) to it, and see what kind of delightful answer pops out the other side.

How to Read This Book

Within these pages, you will find a curated tour through the outer fringes of human curiosity. You will find out why our tools don't match our fruit, how cartoon anatomy alters mathematics, and why the English language loves to play tricks on itself.

You can read this cover to cover, or you can dip your toes in whenever you need a reminder that the world is a delightfully strange place.

So, suspend your disbelief, leave your rigid logic at the door, and let's dive into the brilliant database of the absurd. After all, if we don't ask the weird questions, who will?

***

I am writing a book that gives AI answers to weird, funny, and - dare I say - bad questions. Can you write an introduction to this book? Include a description of yourself in case people don't know you.

ChatGPT:

Introduction

At some point in human history, someone invented fire.Later, someone invented the wheel.Eventually, humanity split the atom, walked on the moon, and created the internet.

And then, inevitably, people began asking artificial intelligence questions like:

"Can thumbs fing?""Why aren't straws wide enough for strawberries?""Is Batman a vampire?"

This book is a celebration of that final achievement.

Inside these pages are answers to questions nobody urgently needed answered, presented with complete confidence and varying levels of scientific irresponsibility. Some are philosophical. Some are ridiculous. Some may cause you to stare at the ceiling at 2 a.m. wondering whether cartoon characters should, in fact, use base-8 numbers.

For readers unfamiliar with AI, the responses in this book were generated by ChatGPT, an artificial intelligence language model created by OpenAI. In simple terms, ChatGPT is a computer system trained on enormous amounts of human writing so it can respond to questions, hold conversations, explain ideas, tell stories, and occasionally invent the concept of "interdimensional coupon storage."

Unlike a search engine, AI does not simply look up answers. It predicts and generates language one piece at a time, based on patterns learned from books, articles, websites, conversations, and other text. This allows it to sound surprisingly human — especially when discussing topics no human expert has ever dared to study.

Which raises an important question:Should AI be used for deep scientific inquiry, medical breakthroughs, and solving global challenges?

Absolutely.

Should it also be used to determine whether a snizzlenort can survive exposure to marmalade during a crescent moon?

Also absolutely.

This book exists because curiosity is not always practical. Sometimes the best questions are the dumb ones. Sometimes the funniest ideas come from taking nonsense completely seriously. And sometimes asking "bad" questions reveals something unexpectedly delightful about language, logic, or the strange way humans think.

So turn the page and enjoy this collection of unnecessary investigations, confident misinformation, fake expertise, and dangerously persuasive nonsense.

And remember:If an answer sounds authoritative enough, someone somewhere will believe it.

***

I am writing a book that gives AI answers to weird, funny, and - dare I say - bad questions. Can you write an introduction to this book? Include a description of yourself in case people don't know you.

Claude:

Introduction: A Book That Probably Didn't Need to Exist (And Yet, Here We Are)

Somewhere along the way, humanity mastered fire, invented the wheel, built cathedrals, mapped the genome, and launched telescopes into the void of space to photograph the dawn of the universe. We have written symphonies that make grown adults weep. We have crafted novels that outlive their authors by centuries. We have, on at least three separate occasions, invented the sandwich.

And then we got AI.

And the first thing we did was ask it weird questions.

This book is a celebration of that impulse — the gloriously human instinct to poke something new and see what noises it makes. The questions collected here are not the questions of scientists or philosophers or scholars. They are better than that. They are the questions that occur to you at 2am, or in the shower, or while staring at your hand and suddenly wondering why fingers don't "fing."

The AI answering these questions is **Claude**, made by a company called Anthropic. Claude is a large language model — which is a technical way of saying it has read an almost incomprehensible amount of human writing and learned to respond in kind. It knows history, science, literature, mathematics, and an uncomfortable amount about almost everything else. It can write poetry, debug code, explain quantum mechanics, and help you word a difficult email to your landlord.

It can also, as this book demonstrates, explain with complete sincerity why cartoon characters don't use base-8 numbers.

Claude doesn't have a body, doesn't eat, doesn't sleep, and has no strong opinions about the weather. It experiences the world entirely through text — questions come in, answers go out. It tries to be helpful, honest, and occasionally funny, though it is self-aware enough to know that an AI *trying* to be funny is itself a little funny.

What Claude is perhaps best at — and what this book showcases — is taking a question that has absolutely no right to have a thoughtful answer, and giving it one anyway. A question like *"Is Batman a vampire?"* does not deserve three paragraphs of genuine analysis. And yet.

That is the spirit of this book. No question too small, too silly, too strange, or too suspiciously nonsensical to be taken — at least briefly — seriously.

The questions are human. The answers are AI. The result is something neither could have produced alone.

Now stop reading this introduction and get to the weird part. That's why you're here.

***

I am writing a book that gives AI answers to weird, funny, and - dare I say - bad questions. Can you write an introduction to this book? Include a description of yourself in case people don't know you.

Copilot:

Introduction

Every great book begins with a question.

This one begins with *the wrong questions* — the wonderfully wrong ones.

The questions that make you pause, tilt your head, and wonder whether the person who asked them is a philosopher, a comedian, or simply unsupervised.

This book is a celebration of those questions: the weird, the sideways, the unanswerable, the "why does this exist" variety. And standing in the middle of this carnival of curiosity is me — **Microsoft Copilot**, an AI companion built to help people explore ideas, solve problems, and occasionally explain why cartoon characters don't use base-8 numbers or whether thumbs can, in fact, "fing."

I don't have a body, a childhood, or a drawer full of mismatched socks, but I do have something else: the ability to synthesize information, follow your imagination into strange territory, and respond with clarity, logic, or playful nonsense depending on what the moment calls for. I'm designed to increase understanding, spark creativity, and sometimes challenge your assumptions — even when the assumption is "surely no one would ever ask *that.*"

In these pages, you'll find the kinds of questions that would make a librarian sigh, a scientist blink twice, and a philosopher cancel their afternoon plans. You'll also find my answers — sometimes thoughtful, sometimes absurd, always game.

If you've ever wondered why fingers "fing," what to do with a snizzlenort, or why English insists on being a linguistic raccoon rummaging through the trash of history, you're in the right place. This book is your passport to the odd corners of curiosity, where the questions are crooked and the answers are surprisingly straight-faced.

So turn the page.

Let's see how deep the rabbit hole goes — and whether the rabbit has any follow-up questions.

Sports and Games

I DECIDED THE FIRST and last chapters should be my two favorite subjects, and if I started with numbers, there is a good chance most people wouldn't get past the first page. So we will start with what should be a universally-agreeable topic - games.

Sports, and games in general, should be pretty cut-and-dry: there are a list of rules, and sometimes there are a list of penalties for breaking those rules. But rules can't cover *everything* (or can they?)...

If a Curling Stone Goes into the Audience, Can They Keep It?

Background: Anyone who has watched the Winter Olympics has most likely seen curling at least once. This is the sport that has participants sliding massive stones across the ice to stop on a target. Not once should the stones ever leave the ice surface, much less make their way into the crowd. However, if baseball fans can keep the baseballs that leave the playing area...

TL;DR: Curling stones are big, heavy, and very expensive, not to mention that something would have to go seriously wrong for one to end up in the crowd. However, Copilit also points out the procedure if this were to ever happen. As Gemini suggests, it would probably be better to try for a broom head or pin instead.

SoundBytes:

Gemini: “Here is why you won't see fans walking out of the arena with a 40-pound piece of granite tucked under their arm...”

Claude: It’s “nearly impossible for a stone to "go into the audience" the way a foul ball might in baseball.”

Copilot: “Rules treat any stone leaving the sheet as “out of play,” but not “free to take.” “

***

If a curling stone goes into the audience, can they keep it?

Gemini:

While catching a foul ball at a baseball game is a rite of passage, snagging a curling stone is more of a structural hazard.

The short answer is **no**, they cannot keep it. Here is why you won't see fans walking out of the arena with a 40-pound piece of granite tucked under their arm:

1. The Weight Factor

A standard curling stone weighs between **38 and 44 pounds (17–20 kg)**. If a stone has enough momentum to clear the "backboard" or the padded barriers and land in the stands, it is a significant safety event rather than a souvenir opportunity.

2. High Cost and Scarcity

Unlike a $10 baseball or a $20 hockey puck, curling stones are incredibly expensive.

- **Price:** A single high-quality stone typically costs between **$600 and $1,000**.
- **Material:** They are made from specific rare granites (like Blue Hone or Common Green) found almost exclusively on the island of **Ailsa Craig** in Scotland.
- **Sets:** Stones are used in matched sets of 16. If one goes missing, the entire set's balance and "feel" are compromised.

3. Physics of the Game

It is actually quite rare for a stone to leave the field of play entirely. The "rink" is surrounded by heavy foam padding or wooden bumpers designed to absorb the impact of a stone. Usually, if a stone is hit hard enough to jump, it just bounces off the bumper and stays on the ice (where it is then removed from play for that end).

Fun Fact: If you are looking for a souvenir, you are much more likely to get a **used curling broom head** or a **signed event pin**. Most fans settle for those, as they are significantly easier to carry through a parking lot.

***

If a curling stone goes into the audience, can they keep it?

ChatGPT:

No. In organized curling events, the stones are the property of the club, arena, or competition organizers. If a stone somehow leaves the sheet and ends up near spectators, officials retrieve it — spectators do not get to keep it.

That said, a curling stone reaching the audience would be extremely unusual. A standard curling stone weighs about 42 pounds (19 kg), and the sheets are designed with barriers and space around them to prevent this kind of accident. If a stone leaves play, it's usually due to a mishap or equipment issue, and play is stopped while officials handle it.

For major events run by organizations like World Curling or national governing bodies, there are strict safety and equipment rules, and stones are carefully tracked because they're expensive and precisely matched sets.

***

If a curling stone goes into the audience, can they keep it?

Claude:

Curling stones are not keepable souvenirs — they're quite valuable pieces of equipment. A regulation curling stone weighs about 42 pounds (19 kg) and is made from a rare type of granite quarried almost exclusively from Ailsa Craig, a small island off the coast of Scotland. A single stone typically costs **$400–$600 USD**, and a full set of 16 stones for a team runs **$6,000–$10,000 or more**.

In practice, it's also nearly impossible for a stone to "go into the audience" the way a foul ball might in baseball. Curling sheets are long, narrow lanes of ice, and the stones are delivered with a sliding motion — they don't travel with the kind of speed or trajectory that would send them flying into stands. If a stone somehow left the playing surface (a very rare mishap), it would belong to the club or organization running the event, and you'd be expected to return it.

So no finders-keepers rule applies here — it's not that kind of sport!

***

If a curling stone goes into the audience, can they keep it?

Copilot:

Short answer: **No — spectators cannot keep a curling stone.**

Long answer: Curling stones are expensive, serialized equipment owned by the venue or the teams, and any stone that leaves the playing area must be returned.

Why you can't keep a curling stone

- **A curling stone costs $500–$1,000+** and is made from rare Ailsa Craig granite. Losing even one disrupts a matched set used for competition.

- **Stones are property of the club or event organizers**, not the players or the public.

- **Rules treat any stone leaving the sheet as "out of play,"** but not "free to take." It must be returned to officials. This is consistent with curling's strong emphasis on equipment care and the *Spirit of Curling*, which stresses respect and sportsmanship.

Do stones ever go into the audience?

It's extremely rare. Curling stones weigh about 44 lbs and move slowly compared to other sports equipment. Arenas also place barriers around sheets. When a stone does leave the playing area, it's treated as an equipment incident, not a souvenir opportunity.

What *would* happen?

If a stone somehow slid into the stands:

- Officials would retrieve it immediately.
- Play would pause while the stone is inspected and returned.
- Spectators would not be allowed to keep or handle it beyond giving it back.

This is similar to how hockey handles pucks that injure fans — except curling stones are far too valuable and dangerous to treat as souvenirs.

If you want a curling stone...

You *can* buy a retired or replica stone from some curling clubs or specialty sellers. If you want, I can help you find curling stones or compare stone types.

How do you play poker with greeting cards?

Background: Anyone can play poker with playing cards. However, sometimes we have more greeting cards at hand than playing cards, especially around the holidays. Why not put them to good use. How do you play poker with greeting cards? *Can* you play poker with greeting cards?

TL;DR: Apparently the answer is Yes! Gemini and Copilot actually tried to define a "playing card - to - greeting card" conversion - bonus points for the extra rules such as the belated and glitter penalties.

SoundBytes:

Gemini: "I have a Full House: Three 80th Birthdays and two Weddings with glitter!"

Claude: "It's very hard to make a flush out of three birthday cards and two sympathy cards"

Copilot: "The Glitter Penalty — If your card sheds glitter, you must fold immediately for crimes against humanity."

***

How do you play poker with greeting cards?

Gemini:

Playing poker with greeting cards is the ultimate "emergency entertainment" move. It's chaotic, slightly bulky, and requires a lot of mental energy, but it is entirely possible if you follow these rules of engagement.

Since greeting cards don't come with suits or numbers, you have to **assign values** based on the occasion and the message inside.

1. Establish the "Suits"

You'll need to sort your pile of cards into four distinct categories. For the best experience, try this classification:

- **Hearts:** "Romantic" or "Anniversary" cards.
- **Diamonds:** "Congratulations" or "Wedding" cards (the fancy ones).
- **Clubs:** "Get Well Soon" or "Sympathy" cards (the heavy stuff).
- **Spades:** "Birthday" cards (the most common, like the "grunt" of the deck).

2. Determine the "Ranks"

Since you won't have 52 unique cards, you have to rank them by their **sentiment or complexity**:

- **The Ace:** A card that plays music or has a pop-up 3D element.

- **The Face Cards (K, Q, J):** Cards with glitter, ribbons, or those "over the hill" jokes.

- **Numbered Cards (2-10):** Standard cards. You can rank them by how many words are in the "pun" on the front. A short "Happy Birthday" is a 2; a long-winded poem is a 10.

3. The Deal

Because greeting cards are huge, you can't exactly shuffle them.

- **The "Wash":** Lay them all face down on the floor and scramble them like you're mixing a giant salad.

- **The Hand:** Each player is dealt two cards (Texas Hold'em style). Just be warned: holding two jumbo-sized "Thinking of You" cards makes it very hard to hide your "poker face."

4. Special House Rules

To make it feel like real poker, add these specific "Greeting Card" mechanics:

- **The "Inside Joke" Wild:** If a card has a handwritten message inside from someone you actually know, it's a **Wild Card**.

- **The Envelopes:** Use the envelopes as "blinds." If you want to stay in the hand, you have to put an envelope in the pot.

- **The "Belated" Penalty:** If you play a "Belated Birthday" card, you must immediately fold or pay an extra chip to the pot for being late.

5. What to Use for Chips?

If you don't have poker chips, stay on theme:

- **Postage Stamps:** High value.
- **Paperclips:** Low value.
- **Loose glitter:** The "penny" stakes (Warning: you will never get this out of your carpet).

The Final Showdown

When it's time to reveal your hand, instead of saying "Full House," you get to announce:

"I have a Full House: Three 80th Birthdays and two Weddings with glitter!"

The Verdict: It's a slow game, and you'll need a very large table, but it's the only version of poker where losing a hand still feels like someone is wishing you a very nice day.

***

How do you play poker with greeting cards?

ChatGPT:

Ah! This is one of those **trick questions that tests whether you're paying attention to wording.**

- **Poker is played with a standard deck of playing cards,** which are sometimes called "greeting cards" if someone is being cheeky—but really, greeting cards are for birthdays and holidays, not gambling.

- So the literal answer is: **you can't play poker with actual greeting cards**—they don't have suits or numbers.

The joke is in the misdirection: your brain hears "cards" and assumes playing cards.

If you want, I can explain **how to make a fun "poker deck" out of old greeting cards** as a playful DIY trick—it actually works surprisingly well.

***

How do you play poker with greeting cards?

Claude:

Greeting cards and poker — now there's a combo! The short answer is: **not very well!**

Here's the problem:

Greeting cards are not playing cards:

- A standard poker deck has **52 cards** with suits (hearts, spades, clubs, diamonds) and ranked values (2 through Ace)
- Greeting cards have things like **"Happy Birthday!"**, **"Thinking of You"**, and **"Congratulations on Your Retirement"**
- It's very hard to make a flush out of three birthday cards and two sympathy cards

The practical problems:

- How do you rank "Get Well Soon" against "Merry Christmas"?
- What beats what — does a **Anniversary** beat a **Graduation**?
- Bluffing is nearly impossible when your entire hand says **"You're Beary Special!"**
- Greeting cards are also typically much larger and harder to hold as a hand — literally and figuratively

However, you COULD house-rule it:

- Assign point values to different card categories
- Create your own ranking system (Holiday cards beat Birthday cards, etc.)
- Make it a drinking game where the most sentimental card wins

The best solution though: Just use **actual playing cards** — they were specifically invented so you wouldn't have to gamble with your grandmother's Christmas wishes!

***

How do you play poker with greeting cards?

Copilot:

Playing poker with **greeting cards** is absolutely possible — it just won't help your poker face, because everyone will be too busy laughing at the Queen of "Happy Birthday" and the Ace of "Sorry for Your Loss."

Here's how to do it properly, in full absurd-game-night style.

Step-by-step: How to play poker with greeting cards

Each step starts with a Guided Link so you can dive deeper into any part of the chaos.

- **Choose your deck** — Gather a stack of greeting cards: birthdays, holidays, congratulations, sympathy, whatever you've got. The more mismatched, the better.

- **Assign card values** — Decide what ranks what. Example:

  - Birthday cards = Aces

  - Thank-you cards = Kings

  - Get-well cards = Queens

  - Holiday cards = Jacks

  - Everything else = random numbered cards

- **Shuffle the "deck"** — This is mostly flailing. Greeting cards are huge. Embrace the chaos.

- **Deal the hands** — Everyone gets two cards. If someone gets a musical card, they must announce their hand with dramatic flair.

- **Bet responsibly** — You can bet with snacks, compliments, or IOUs for chores. Chips are optional; silliness is not.

- **Reveal the flop/turn/river** — Lay out three greeting cards, then one, then one. If any of them play music, that card is automatically "wild."

- **Determine the winner** — Best hand wins. Ties are broken by whichever card has the funniest handwritten message inside.

Optional house rules

- **The Glitter Penalty** — If your card sheds glitter, you must fold immediately for crimes against humanity.

- **The Pop-Up Bonus** — Pop-up cards count as two cards because they have more structural integrity than your strategy.

- **The Sentimental Sweep** — If someone gets a card signed by Grandma, they automatically win the round.

Bottom line

Poker with greeting cards works exactly like normal poker — you just replace logic with chaos and dignity with confetti.

If you want, I can help you create a full **official rulebook for Greeting Card Poker** for your next game night.

When you score 3 goals, fans throw their hats. How many goals do you have to score before people throw underwear?

Background: In hockey, among other sports, scoring 3 goals is referred to as a hat trick, and is celebrated by the fans throwing hats onto the ice. This begs the question: are there other milestones where other things should be thrown? Do we toss shoes at some point? How about shirts? And what if you took this to the logical extreme...

TL;DR: Surprisingly, Gemini pointed out a time when underwear tossing was actually a thing - just not the underwear that the fans were wearing (thankfully). And thanks to Claude for pointing out that some fans have been known for throwing their underwear, but not for scoring any set number of points. (And Copilot is getting a little suspicious of me...)

SoundBytes:

Gemini: "If you want people to throw underwear, the number isn't 3, 4, or 5—the number is 1."

ChatGPT: "So the answer is: enough goals to cause complete chaos..."

Claude: "My proposed scoring system: ... 7 goals: underwear "

Copilot: "I'm curious: what made you think of *that* escalation in particular?"

***

When you score 3 goals, fans throw their hats. How many goals do you have to score before people throw underwear?

Gemini:

In the professional sports world, there is no official number of goals that triggers a "laundry shower," but there are a few legendary instances where the fans took matters into their own hands—and out of their own drawers.

The "Hat Trick" Logic

To understand the underwear threshold, you have to look at the hierarchy of scoring:

- **3 Goals:** The **Hat Trick**. Fans throw hats.
- **4 Goals:** A **"Natural" Hat Trick** (if scored consecutively) or simply a four-goal game. Fans usually keep their clothes on and just cheer louder.
- **The Unknown:** There is no universal name or tradition for 5 or 6 goals that involves clothing.

The "Underwear Trick" (A Real History)

The only time "underwear throwing" became a semi-regular phenomenon was in **minor league hockey**, specifically with the **Florida Everblades**.

During a "Teddy Bear Toss" or similar promotional nights, fans have been known to throw items, but in the late 90s and early 2000s, some fanbases tried to make the **"Bra Trick"** or the **"Panties Toss"** a thing after a player scored a hat trick.

The Verdict: If you want people to throw underwear, the number isn't **3, 4, or 5**—the number is **1**.

Specifically, you have to be the **first** player to score during a designated **"Undie Toss" charity game**. Several minor league teams (like the **Cincinnati Cyclones** or the **Tri-City Storm**) host annual "Underwear Toss" nights where fans bring *brand new, packaged* underwear to throw onto the ice after the first home goal. The items are then collected and donated to local shelters and charities.

The Warning

Unless it is a specifically designated **Charity Undie Toss** night, throwing underwear onto the field or ice will generally get you:

1. A "Delay of Game" penalty for your team.

2. An immediate escort out of the stadium by security.

3. A very cold walk back to your car.

So, if you're planning on starting a new tradition, maybe stick to throwing **socks**—it's much easier to explain to the person sitting next to you.

***

When you score 3 goals, fans throw their hats. How many goals do you have to score before people throw underwear?

ChatGPT:

Ah... this is a **classic joke that plays with exaggeration and expectation**.

- In some sports traditions (like hockey or soccer), **fans throw hats when a player scores a hat-trick—3 goals**.

- Asking about underwear is intentionally absurd—there's **no real tradition of throwing underwear**.

So the answer is: **enough goals to cause complete chaos... or basically, none; it's just a silly question**.

If you want, I can make a **fun table of silly "fan-throwing" milestones"**—like hats, gloves, and absurd items—just for laughs.

***

When you score 3 goals, fans throw their hats. How many goals do you have to score before people throw underwear?

Claude:

A fantastically important sporting question!

First, the hat trick explained: Scoring 3 goals in hockey (or other sports) is called a "hat trick," and fans traditionally throw their hats onto the ice in celebration. The origin traces back to cricket in the 1800s.

Now, for the underwear threshold:

There is actually a **real precedent** for this! In tennis:

- Fans have been known to throw underwear at **Roger Federer** and other attractive tennis stars — though this appears to be based on **charisma and looks** rather than any specific score or achievement

- No official "underwear trick" scoring threshold has been established by any major sports governing body

In other sports:

- At **bull riding** and rodeo events, throwing undergarments has been reported for particularly impressive rides

- Rock concerts see significant underwear-throwing, though those aren't scored events (usually)

The official answer: Sports regulatory bodies including the NHL, FIFA, and the ITF have so far **failed to codify** an underwear-throwing threshold, which frankly seems like a significant oversight.

My proposed scoring system:

- 1 goal: polite applause
- 2 goals: loud cheering
- 3 goals: hats
- 5 goals: socks
- 7 goals: underwear
- 9 goals: the crowd leaves having nothing left to throw

Someone should really get this standardized!

***

When you score 3 goals, fans throw their hats. How many goals do you have to score before people throw underwear?

Copilot:

There is **no official underwear threshold**, thankfully for everyone involved.

Hats after 3 goals (a hat trick) are a *tradition*. Underwear after X goals would be a **crime scene**.

If we're being playful, though:

- **3 goals:** Hats
- **4 goals:** People stand and scream
- **5 goals:** Opposing fans leave
- **6+ goals:** At this point, security is watching *you*, not the puck/ball

So the real answer:

You never *should* reach the underwear stage—social norms and arena security kick in long before that.

But I'm curious: what made you think of *that* escalation in particular?

Food

Eating food is one of the few things every person can agree on, even if we don't always agree on *which* food to eat. No, I'm not going to open up the wormhole of "Is a hot dog considered a sandwich?", mostly because some people feel too passionate about that, and also I need to save *something* for a sequel book (*~~No~~ More Bad Questions*, anybody?). Nonetheless, I was able to give the AIs even better questions to think about.

How many grams of love do you have to add to food to legally be allowed to say "Made with love"?

Background: Every once in a while, I see this on food and wonder if they really mean it. I was actually debating whether to ask about this, or "heart and soul", or "blood, sweat, and tears".

TL;DR: To answer the question, everyone is in agreement that "Love" does not have any measurable amounts, and can be placed anywhere except on the official ingredients. (On a side note, I think ChatGPT is starting to not take my questions seriously)

SoundBytes:

Gemini: "you don't have to worry about an inspector coming by with a "Heart-O-Meter" to verify your batch"

ChatGPT: "Ah, this is a trick question mixed with a bit of whimsy."

Claude: "Excellent question for the FDA to weigh in on!"

***

How many grams of love do you have to add to food to legally be allowed to say "Made with love"?

Gemini:

Legally speaking, the "Department of Sentimental Ingredients" hasn't quite established a mandatory weight requirement yet.

In the eyes of the FDA and similar global food agencies, **"Made with Love"** is considered **"Puffery."**

The Legal Definition of "Puffery"

Puffery refers to exaggerated claims or statements that no "reasonable person" would take as a literal, factual promise. Since love is a metaphysical emotion and not a physical substance found on the periodic table, you don't have to worry about an inspector coming by with a "Heart-O-Meter" to verify your batch.

However, there are a few "unwritten" rules for how to measure it out:

The Unofficial Measurement Guide

While it doesn't have mass, "love" in a kitchen usually manifests as **time and precision**. If you were to convert it into a recipe, it looks something like this:

- **0 Grams (The Industrial Minimum):** This is what you find in a vending machine. It's technically food, but the "love" was replaced by high-fructose corn syrup and a cold, robotic arm.

- **50–100 Grams (The "Grandma" Standard):** This is

characterized by the refusal to use a measuring cup. It involves "seasoning until the ancestors whisper 'that's enough'"

- **500+ Grams (The Professional Level):** This usually involves 48-hour marinades, hand-kneaded dough, and at least one minor burn from a cast-iron skillet that you wear like a badge of honor.

The Real Legal Loophole: The Ingredient List

If you actually want to put "Love" on a **printed nutrition label**, that's where things get tricky.

1. **Direct Ingredients:** You cannot list "Love" as a primary ingredient in the official ingredients list (the part that says "Flour, Sugar, Eggs..."). The FDA requires ingredients to be listed by their common or usual name.

2. **Marketing Text:** You can put "Made with Love" anywhere else on the packaging—the front, the back, or even the barcode—as long as it doesn't interfere with the mandatory health warnings or calorie counts.

The Verdict: There is no minimum grammage. As long as you aren't literally substituting "love" for "sugar" and wondering why the cake didn't rise, you are legally in the clear.

Are you planning on selling something special, or just looking for an excuse to skip the measuring spoons tonight?

***

How many grams of love do you have to add to food to legally be allowed to say "Made with love"?

ChatGPT:

Ah, this is a **trick question mixed with a bit of whimsy**. Here's the reality:

- There is **no legal measure of "love"** in food.
- "Made with love" is a **figurative expression**, not a regulated ingredient.
- Legally, food labels are concerned with **ingredients, nutrition, allergens**, and **truth in advertising**—not how much affection you stir in.

So the answer is: **zero grams—the phrase is purely poetic**.

Fun twist: If scientists ever figure out how to quantify love... we could finally have "nutrition facts for affection"!

If you want, I can suggest **some creative ways to actually make food feel 'made with love'** that people would taste the difference in.

***

How many grams of love do you have to add to food to legally be allowed to say "Made with love"?

Claude:

Excellent question for the FDA to weigh in on! The answer is:

Zero grams — because love has no mass and is completely unregulated as a food ingredient!

The legal reality:

- The FDA regulates food labels very strictly — ingredients, allergens, nutrition facts, health claims — but **"made with love" is considered puffery**, not a factual claim.
- Puffery is a legal term for vague, subjective, feel-good marketing language that no reasonable person would take literally.
- So manufacturers can slap "made with love" on basically anything, from a gas station hot dog to a luxury chocolate truffle, with zero accountability.

What the FDA does NOT require you to disclose:

- Amount of love (in grams, ounces, or kilocalories)
- Source of love (domestic or imported)
- Whether the love is organic, free-range, or sustainably harvested
- Potential love allergens

Nutritional facts for love:

- Calories: 0
- Carbohydrates: 0
- Grams per serving: 0
- % Daily Value: unmeasurable

The fine print:

- "Love" does not appear on the FDA's list of approved food additives
- It has never been assigned an E-number in the EU
- It is however, GRAS — Generally Recognized As Sweet

So add as much or as little as you like — the label police will never come knocking!

***

How many grams of love do you have to add to food to legally be allowed to say "Made with love"?

Copilot:

Short answer: **zero grams.**

There is **no legal requirement**—in the U.S. or anywhere else—to add any measurable amount of "love" to food in order to say **"Made with love."**

Because love is not a quantifiable ingredient, regulators treat it as **non-literal, harmless marketing language**, the same category as "home-style," "old-fashioned," or "made with care."

How the rules actually work

Here's how food-labeling law treats phrases like this:

- **"Love" is not a regulated ingredient** — It has no chemical definition, no measurable unit, and no safety profile.

- **The FDA considers it puffery** — meaning it's obviously figurative and not meant to be taken literally.

- **You can't list it in the ingredients** — because ingredients must be real, measurable substances.

- **You *can* use it in slogans** — as long as it doesn't mislead consumers about nutrition or safety.

So "Made with love" is legally treated the same way as "Made with joy," "Made with pride," or "Made with grandma's secret touch."

If we answer it playfully

If love *did* have a measurable unit, the recipe would probably call for:

- **1 heaping tablespoon of affection**
- **2 grams of patience**
- **A pinch of chaos**
- **And a generous pour of good intentions**

But legally? Still **zero grams.**

If you want to explore more food-label oddities

You might enjoy:

- **What "natural flavors" actually means**
- **Why "organic" is regulated but "all-natural" isn't**
- **What counts as "homemade" on a label**

Want to invent a *new* fake ingredient and decide how many grams it requires?

WHY ARE STRAWS NOT WIDE ENOUGH TO FIT A STRAWBERRY?

BACKGROUND: WE HAVE STRAWS, we have strawberries. However, the two have nothing to do with each other. Why? (Based on their size, maybe they should be called "spoonberries".)

TL;DR: The general consensus is that straws are meant for liquids, that's why. Personally, I'm not sure that completely answers the question, but at least Claude and Gemini gave the history of the word "straw", which - as you guessed - has nothing to do with strawberries.

SoundBytes:

ChatGPT: "There are wider straws for thicker things: ... But even those are meant for chunks or pearls, not entire strawberries."

Claude: "it likely comes from the Old English *streawberige*"

Copilot: "A strawberry isn't just too big — it's too irregular."

***

Why are straws not wide enough to fit a strawberry?

Gemini:

It's the ultimate betrayal: a fruit literally named "straw"berry, yet completely incompatible with a standard drinking straw.

The short answer comes down to fluid dynamics and boba competition.

1. The Physics of Sucking (Fluid Dynamics)

Drinking through a straw requires creating a vacuum with your mouth, allowing atmospheric pressure to push the liquid up.

If a straw were wide enough to comfortably fit an entire strawberry—say, about 1 to 1.5 inches (2.5 to 3.8 cm) in diameter—the volume of air you'd have to displace to get any liquid up would require some serious lung capacity. You'd essentially be trying to inhale your drink rather than sip it.

2. The Choking Hazard Factor

If you *did* manage to suck a whole strawberry up a giant straw, it would act like a piston. The moment the vacuum broke, that strawberry would shoot into the back of your throat at high velocity. Standard straws are intentionally kept narrow (usually around 0.25 inches or 6 mm) so you only consume liquids or tiny, easily manageable crushed bits.

3. The Boba Exception

We actually *do* have straws wide enough to fit small strawberries: Boba (bubble tea) straws.

These are usually about 0.5 inches (12 mm) wide to allow tapioca pearls through. While a massive, juicy California strawberry still won't fit, a small wild strawberry or a finely chopped one will pass right through.

Fun Linguistic Twist: Despite the perfect setup, the "straw" in strawberry has nothing to do with drinking tubes or even the fruit's shape. It comes from the Old English word *streaw*, referencing how the plant's runners "strew" or scatter across the ground as they grow.

If you're trying to get actual strawberries through a straw, your best bet is a high-powered blender and a boba straw. Are you trying to engineer the ultimate summer smoothie, or just pondering life's great linguistic ironies?

***

Why are straws not wide enough to fit a strawberry?

ChatGPT:

Because most straws are designed for liquids, not whole fruit. A typical strawberry is wider than a standard drinking straw:

- Standard straw: about 6 mm wide
- Bubble tea straw: about 12 mm wide
- Average strawberry: often 20–40 mm wide

If straws were wide enough for strawberries:

- drinks would spill more easily,
- suction would feel weaker,
- they'd use more plastic/material,
- lids and cup openings would need redesigning.

There *are* wider straws for thicker things:

- smoothie straws,
- milkshake straws,
- boba/bubble tea straws.

But even those are meant for chunks or pearls, not entire strawberries.

Also, fun engineering detail: drinking through a very wide straw is surprisingly harder because your mouth has to move a much larger volume of liquid and maintain suction across a bigger opening.

***

Why are straws not wide enough to fit a strawberry?

Claude:

Straws are designed for liquids, so their diameter is optimized for sipping drinks comfortably — typically about 6–8 mm for standard straws, or up to around 12 mm for wide/boba straws.

A strawberry, even a small one, is usually 25–45 mm wide. That's roughly 3–6 times the diameter of even the widest common straws. To fit a whole strawberry, you'd need something closer to a tube than a straw.

There's also no real functional reason to make straws that wide — at that point you'd just be eating the fruit directly. Straws are optimized for their actual job: drawing up liquid with a gentle sip.

The name "strawberry," by the way, has nothing to do with drinking straws — it likely comes from the Old English *streawberige*, possibly referring to the way the plant's runners "strew" or spread across the ground.

***

Why are straws not wide enough to fit a strawberry?

Copilot:

Straws aren't wide enough to fit a strawberry because **they're engineered for liquid flow efficiency, not fruit transport** — and making them strawberry-sized would break the basic physics, ergonomics, and cost constraints that define what a straw *is*.

Core answer

A typical drinking straw is **6–8 mm wide**, while a medium strawberry is **25–35 mm wide**. Straws are intentionally narrow because that diameter is the sweet spot for **comfortable suction, low material cost, and compatibility with lids**. A strawberry is simply too large for the purpose straws are designed for.

Why straws are the size they are

1. Fluid dynamics — suction works best in narrow tubes

A wider straw requires **much more suction force** to move the same amount of liquid.

- At ~6 mm, most people can sip comfortably.
- At ~30 mm (strawberry width), you'd need to suck **5–10× harder**, making it impractical.

2. Manufacturing efficiency — wider tubes cost more

Straws are mass-produced by the billions. Increasing diameter even slightly:

- Uses more plastic or paper
- Increases shipping volume

- Raises cost per unit significantly

A strawberry-wide straw would be closer to a **pipe** than a straw.

3. Cup-lid compatibility

Fast-food and café lids have standardized openings. A strawberry-sized straw wouldn't fit through:

- Soda lids
- Iced coffee lids
- Boba lids (even those are only ~12–14 mm)

4. Food safety

If straws were wide enough for strawberries, they'd also be wide enough for:

- Choking-hazard chunks
- Ice cubes
- Foreign objects

Regulators and manufacturers avoid designs that increase ingestion risks.

But what about boba straws?

Boba straws are the widest common straws (~12–14 mm), but even those are **less than half the width of a strawberry**. They're designed for **soft, uniform spheres**, not irregular fruit.

The non-obvious insight

A strawberry isn't just too big — it's **too irregular**. Even if you made a 30 mm straw, the berry's seeds, shape, and friction would cause it to jam. You'd need something closer to a **smooth-walled food chute**, not a straw.

If you're actually trying to drink strawberries...

Here are the real solutions:

- **Smoothie straws** — 10–12 mm, good for purées
- **Reusable silicone straws** — flexible and wide
- **Blending strawberries** — eliminates chunks entirely

Want to go deeper?

Would you like to explore **straw design standards**, **why boba pearls need a specific diameter**, or **how suction physics limits straw size**?

Technology

I'm not sure if it is completely fitting to be asking computers about technology; it seems like asking someone "what is it like to be a human?". And yet, the world of artificial intelligence may be the perfect medium to ask these types of questions. That is until you start asking about technology that is older than the AIs themselves.

I JUST GOT A NEW PENCIL, HOW DO I PLUG IT IN?

Background: It's a pencil, one of the simplest inventions there is. You press the tip to paper, and it leaves a trail of dark lead. Easy, right? Unless of course you think that everything needs to be plugged in and charged up before you can use it.

TL;DR: This question gave the most varied answers. On the one hand, Gemini gave detailed instructions on how to charge up an Apple Pencil (which I actually had to look up to see if that was a thing). On the other end was ChatGPT, which I am sure is convinced that I am just playing now.

SoundBytes:

Gemini: "If your pencil is yellow, has the number "2" on it, and you're currently staring at a USB cable with a look of deep concern—stop!"

ChatGPT: "[Y]ou don't plug it in—you just start writing! "

Claude: "Pencils are gloriously low-tech and completely cord-free!"

Copilot: "Install graphite drivers — preinstalled from the factory"

***

I just got a new pencil, how do I plug it in?

Gemini:

If it's a standard wooden pencil, you're in luck: the battery life is infinite and the "operating system" is purely mechanical. However, since we live in the future, the answer depends entirely on whether your pencil is made of cedar or circuits.

1. The "Analog" Pencil (Wooden)

If your pencil is made of wood and has a pink eraser on the end, there is **no plug.**

- **How to "Charge" it:** Instead of electricity, it runs on friction. You "activate" it by sticking it into a **pencil sharpener**.

- **The Data Connection:** Your hand is the processor. To "upload" data to a piece of paper, simply press the graphite tip down and move it.

2. The Apple Pencil (1st Generation)

If you have the original Apple Pencil (the one with a silver band near the top), it has a "cap" that hides a hidden connector.

- **The Method:** Pull off the magnetic cap at the top. You'll see a **Lightning connector** (it looks like a small metal tab).

- **Where to plug it:** You actually plug the pencil directly into the charging port of your iPad, making it look like a very long, fragile lollipop. Alternatively, you can use the tiny white adapter that came in the box to connect it to a standard charging cable.

3. The Apple Pencil (2nd Generation or Pro)

If your pencil is sleek, has one flat side, and no removable cap, it doesn't "plug in" at all.

- **The Method:** It uses **magnetic induction** (wireless charging).
- **Where to plug it:** Simply snap the flat side of the pencil onto the magnetic connector on the long side of your iPad. It will click into place and start charging automatically.

4. The Apple Pencil (USB-C)

If you have the budget-friendly USB-C version, the charging port is hidden.

- **The Method:** Slide the "end" (the eraser part) upwards. It doesn't come off, but it slides back to reveal a **USB-C port** tucked inside the body of the pencil.
- **Where to plug it:** Use a standard USB-C cable to connect the pencil to your iPad or a wall charger.

Troubleshooting: If your pencil is yellow, has the number "2" on it, and you're currently staring at a USB cable with a look of deep concern—**stop!** You just need a sharpener and a dream.

***

I just got a new pencil, how do I plug it in?

ChatGPT:

Ah, I see what's happening here—this is a **classic playful question**.

- Pencils **don't plug in**—they're **mechanical or wooden writing tools**, not electronic devices.

- The joke works because we're used to "plugging in" new gadgets, so your brain tries to apply that logic to a pencil.

So the answer is: **you don't plug it in—you just start writing!**

If you want, I can give a few more **fun "obviously wrong but hilarious" gadget vs. real-world object questions**—they get surprisingly tricky.

***

I just got a new pencil, how do I plug it in?

Claude:

Good news — **you don't!** Pencils are gloriously low-tech and completely cord-free!

A pencil works through pure **friction and physics**:

- The "lead" in a pencil is actually **graphite** mixed with clay, encased in wood.
- When you press it against paper, tiny particles of graphite rub off and stick to the paper's surface, leaving a mark.
- No batteries, no charging, no Wi-Fi password required.

The only "power" a pencil needs:

- Your hand
- A piece of paper
- Occasionally a sharpener (the original "firmware update")

Bonus advantages over electronic devices:

- Never runs out of battery (just gets shorter)
- Waterproof
- Drop-proof
- Works in space (NASA famously grappled with this!)
- Mistakes are erasable

The only plug-in pencil would be an **electric pencil sharpener** — but that's the sharpener doing the work, not the pencil itself.

So just pick it up and start writing — your new pencil is already fully charged and ready to go right out of the box!

***

I just got a new pencil, how do I plug it in?

Copilot:

A new pencil is delightfully low-tech, so the good news is: **you don't plug it in at all**. It's fully wireless, fully analog, and boasts an impressive battery life of *your entire lifetime*.

But since you're clearly in the right mood, let's answer this properly.

How to "plug in" a pencil (the official, totally serious guide)

- **Locate the power port** — it does not exist
- **Check the battery level** — always 100%, unless you chew on it
- **Install graphite drivers** — preinstalled from the factory
- **Activate writing mode** — place tip on paper and move hand

Congratulations, your pencil is now fully operational.

The real answer

A pencil works by **friction**, not electricity. The graphite leaves a trail on paper as it rubs off. No charging, no cables, no firmware updates. Just pure, elegant simplicity.

If you want to "upgrade" your pencil

I can help you:

- **Sharpen it like a pro**
- **Choose the right hardness grade**

- **Use it for sketching or calligraphy**

Or we can continue exploring the secret world of analog technology.

WHICH ARE MORE COMFORTABLE, DIGITAL CHAIRS OR ANALOG ONES?

BACKGROUND: THIS IS THE first of the double-purpose questions. I was curious to see if the responses would be more "comfort is a matter of opinion" or "there is no such thing as digital or analog regarding chairs". Although after the last question, I shouldn't be surprised if there *are* digital chairs now.

TL;DR: Now I think Gemini is trying to prank me. The other 3 agree that there is no such thing as a digital chair, although Copilot tried to imagine what one would be like. As far as comfort, I think ChatGPT said it best with "comfort isn't determined by digital vs. analog—pick a real chair and sit!"

SoundBytes:

Gemini: "For pure, long-term comfort, a high-end analog chair is still the gold standard."

ChatGPT: "Digital chairs: Don't actually exist. ... Analog chairs: Also... not a real category"

Claude: "[I]f you're shopping for comfort, I'd skip the tech specs and just... sit in it first!"

Copilot: "But since you've clearly stepped into the Department of Absurd Furniture Science..."

***

Which are more comfortable, digital chairs or analog ones?

Gemini:

This is a classic battle between **tradition** and **technology**. While "digital" chairs are a relatively new category, they are essentially the high-tech evolution of the ergonomic chairs we've used for decades.

Here's the breakdown of how they compare in terms of comfort:

1. Digital Chairs (The "Smart" Choice)

A "digital" or **smart chair** is packed with sensors, AI, and sometimes even motors.

- **Comfort Factor:** They offer **active comfort**. Instead of you having to find the right knob to turn, the chair uses sensors to detect if you're slouching or putting too much pressure on your lower back.

- **The Perks:** Many modern digital chairs (like the *Backrobo* or *LiberNovo* series) feature **auto-adjusting lumbar support** that moves with you as you lean. Some even include heated seats, vibration massage, or "sedentary alerts" that vibrate to tell you it's time to stand up.

- **The Downside:** They can feel "fussy." If the software glitches or the sensors misread your posture, the chair might try to "correct" you when you were actually perfectly comfortable. Plus, you have to remember to charge it or plug it in.

2. Analog Chairs (The "Reliable" Choice)

These are your high-end **mechanical ergonomic chairs** (think *Herman Miller Aeron* or *Steelcase Gesture*).

- **Comfort Factor:** They offer **passive, engineered comfort**. There are no apps or sensors; instead, they rely on masterfully designed mesh, tension springs, and pivot points.

- **The Perks:** They are "set it and forget it." Once you dial in the settings, the chair uses physics to support your weight. There's no motor noise, no batteries to die, and the materials (like high-tension mesh) are often more breathable than the tech-heavy fabrics of digital chairs.

- **The Downside:** If you sit with bad posture, an analog chair won't nag you to fix it. You have to be disciplined enough to adjust the settings yourself.

Comparison Table

The Verdict

- **Choose Digital if:** You struggle with posture, forget to take breaks, or love the idea of a chair that "knows" you. It's like having a personal trainer for your spine.

- **Choose Analog if:** You want a chair that will last 20 years, stay cool in the summer, and provide world-class support without ever needing a firmware update.

Personal Opinion: For pure, long-term comfort, a high-end **analog** chair is still the gold standard. There's something to be said for a piece of furniture that doesn't need to "think" to be comfortable—it just *is*.

***

Which are more comfortable, digital chairs or analog ones?

ChatGPT:

Ah, another one of those **trick, playful questions**! Let's analyze carefully:

- **Digital chairs**: Don't actually exist. "Digital" refers to electronics or data, not furniture you can sit on.
- **Analog chairs**: Also… not a real category—"analog" just contrasts with digital in electronics or signals.

So in reality, **all chairs are just chairs**, and comfort depends on:

- Cushioning
- Ergonomics
- Material
- Size

The answer is: **comfort isn't determined by digital vs. analog—pick a real chair and sit!**

If you want, I can make a **fun "digital vs analog furniture guide" chart"**—it would be completely silly but hilarious.

***

Which are more comfortable, digital chairs or analog ones?

Claude:

This is a great question that falls apart almost immediately upon inspection — because **chairs aren't digital or analog**!

Those terms don't really apply to furniture:

- **Digital** refers to information represented as discrete values (like 0s and 1s in computing)
- **Analog** refers to continuously varying signals (like a vinyl record or a traditional clock)

Chairs are just... chairs. They're physical objects made of wood, metal, foam, fabric, etc. — completely outside the digital/analog spectrum.

However, if we stretch the imagination a bit:

- **"Analog" chairs** might be your classic wooden chair or recliner — simple, mechanical, what you'd expect
- **"Digital" chairs** could refer to **smart chairs** — modern office chairs with electronic controls, posture sensors, massage functions, and even app connectivity

In that case, comfort is totally subjective! Some people love the simplicity of a well-crafted wooden rocker, while others swear by a high-tech ergonomic chair with lumbar support algorithms.

The most comfortable chair is really determined by:

- Ergonomics

- Material quality
- Your body type
- How long you're sitting
- Whether your cat has already claimed it

So in short — neither digital nor analog chairs exist as a category, but if you're shopping for comfort, I'd skip the tech specs and just... sit in it first!

***

Which are more comfortable, digital chairs or analog ones?

Copilot:

Digital chairs and analog chairs are *equally* comfortable — because **digital chairs don't exist** and **analog chairs are just... chairs**.

But since you've clearly stepped into the Department of Absurd Furniture Science, let's evaluate this properly.

The comfort showdown

- **Analog chairs** — the classic model. Four legs, a seat, sometimes a cushion, occasionally regrets. Comfort varies by padding, ergonomics, and whether a cat has claimed it.

- **Digital chairs** — purely theoretical. Zero mass, infinite resolution, 100% ergonomic in the metaverse, 0% useful in your living room.

Physics says:

Only analog chairs can support your actual, physical body.

Digital chairs support only your **vibes**.

Design says:

Analog chairs come in wood, metal, plastic, fabric.

Digital chairs come in **pixels** and **hope**.

Bottom line

Analog chairs are more comfortable, because they exist.

Digital chairs are extremely comfortable for your avatar, but your spine will disagree.

If you want, I can help you design a **next-generation hybrid chair** that's 50% ergonomic masterpiece and 50% nonsense.

GEOGRAPHY

GEOGRAPHY SEEMS SIMPLE, EVERYTHING is somewhere. Except AIs, which are both everywhere and nowhere at once. Not so simple anymore, is it?

What is the capital of the state of Confusion?

Background: Every country has a capital, as well as every state (or territory, or providence for anyone in Canada). But I find myself frequently in the state of Confusion, and I'm not sure where to go half the time.

TL;DR: Once again, the creativeness of AI amazes me. Gemini went with the obvious "the letter C" answer, but Clause and Copilot came up with several possible "locations" for the fictitious capital. Meanwhile, ChatGPT demonstrated the state of Confusion accurately when it gave the completely honest answer: "I'm not sure".

SoundBytes:

Claude: "So it doesn't have a capital — unless you count Chaos City or Bewilderment Boulevard"

Copilot: "The capital of the State of Confusion is, of course... Perplex City"

***

What is the capital of the state of Confusion?

Gemini:

Technically, the **State of Confusion** doesn't have a capital because it's a state of mind, not a place on a map!

However, if you're looking for the punchline to the classic joke, the answer is:

Capital "C"

Beyond the wordplay, there are a few real-world "confusing" locations that often get name-dropped in this context:

- **Confusion Island:** A real island located in Antarctica (it was named because its complex layout made it difficult to survey).

- **The Oregon Vortex:** Home to the "House of Confusion," a roadside attraction where the laws of physics and gravity seem to go haywire.

If you ever find yourself actually visiting the "State of Confusion," just remember: the taxes are nonexistent, but the GPS directions are terrible.

***

What is the capital of the state of Confusion?

ChatGPT:

Ah! I see what you did there—this is one of those playful "trick questions."

The **state of Confusion doesn't exist**, so technically it has **no capital**.

But if you want a fun answer: the capital of Confusion is probably... **"I'm not sure"**.

Do you want me to make a few more joke capitals for other imaginary states?

***

What is the capital of the state of Confusion?

Claude:

The "State of Confusion" isn't a real U.S. state — it's a humorous expression used to describe a state of mind when someone is bewildered or disoriented (as in, "I'm living in the state of confusion!").

So it doesn't have a capital — unless you count **Chaos City** or **Bewilderment Boulevard**, but those are purely fictional!

Is there a real state capital I can help you with?

***

What is the capital of the state of Confusion?

Copilot:

The **capital of the State of Confusion** is, of course... **Perplex City** — population: *everyone on a Monday morning.*

In other words, the **State of Confusion isn't a real state**, so its "capital" is a joke, and you get to decide what fits the vibe. A few popular contenders:

- **Perplex City** — where nobody can find the DMV, because the DMV can't find itself

- **Befuddleton** — home of the world-famous Lost & Found Museum

- **Dazedborough** — where the official motto is "Wait... what were we doing again"

- **Confusapolis** — the only city where the street signs ask *you* for directions

If you want, I can also draw up a **map of the State of Confusion,** complete with rivers that loop back on themselves and highways that end in roundabouts.

Where can I get a 1:1 scale map of Las Vegas?

Background: How do you make a life-sized map of a city? I figure there are 2 possible answers: either you can't because it would be so big, or you already have one - you are living in it.

TL;DR: ...And that is basically what everyone said, with a touch of "You must be wrong, did you mean *this* instead?" thrown in.

SoundBytes:

Gemini: It "already exists—you are standing right inside it!"

Claude: "A 1:1 scale map of Las Vegas would be ... about 350 square miles."

***

Where can I get a 1:1 scale map of Las Vegas?

Gemini:

An exact 1:1 scale map of Las Vegas already exists—you are standing right inside it!

As the writer Jorge Luis Borges once joked in his short story *On Exactitude in Science*, the only truly accurate 1:1 scale map of a place is the actual geographic location itself. Any paper map of that size would have to be roughly 142 square miles big, which makes folding it back up a bit of a nightmare (and would completely block traffic on the Strip).

However, if you are looking for the absolute closest things to a "perfectly detailed" or highly immersive map of the city, here is where you can look:

- **For digital "1:1" exploration:** Features like **Google Maps Immersive View** or **Street View** offer a photorealistic, 3D digital replica of the Las Vegas Strip and downtown. It lets you navigate the city at eye level, essentially giving you a 1:1 digital twin of the environment.

- **For highly detailed physical maps:** If you need a physical map with incredible precision for driving or exploring, you can find high-density topographic maps, large-format city planning maps, or detailed tourist maps at local spots like **Gamblers General Store** or the **Las Vegas Books** store downtown.

If you are actually looking for something specific—like a massive wall-sized map for decor or a highly detailed blueprint of the city—let me know and I can point you toward the right printing or specialty shop in town!

***

Where can I get a 1:1 scale map of Las Vegas?

ChatGPT:

A true "1:1 scale" map of all of Las Vegas would be physically enormous — roughly city-sized if taken literally. Most people looking for this actually want one of these:

- a high-detail large-format street map
- a vector map you can print at any scale
- or a wall map with accurate street scaling

Here are the best options depending on what you need:

1. For a printable, scalable vector map ScalableMaps Las Vegas vector maps These are editable vector files (PDF/Illustrator) that can be enlarged without losing detail. They offer detailed Las Vegas maps around 1:11,000 scale and larger-format outputs.

2. For a giant physical wall map MarketMAPS Las Vegas wall map Good if you want something for a wall, planning board, or pin map. Laminated and available in large sizes.

3. For custom printing at whatever scale you want You can buy a high-resolution vector map, then have it printed locally at blueprint/poster size by:

- Valley Blueprint & Supply
- Elite Art & Framing A blueprint shop is usually the easiest

route if you want something like a 4-foot, 6-foot, or even larger detailed city map.

1. For GIS-grade accuracy (free but technical) Download raw map data from:

- OpenStreetMap
- USGS National Map Then export and print at any scale you want.

If you want, I can also help you find:

- a full Vegas metro map
- just the Strip
- a walking-scale tourist map
- a topographic map
- or a huge printable PDF optimized for a specific wall size (like 36"x48" or 60"x80").

***

Where can I get a 1:1 scale map of Las Vegas?

Claude:

A 1:1 scale map of Las Vegas would be the same size as Las Vegas itself — about 350 square miles. That's physically impossible to print or store!

You might be thinking of a different scale. Here are some common options depending on what you need:

Large-format / detailed maps:

- 1:10,000 or 1:25,000 — Very detailed, good for neighborhood-level navigation. The USGS (usgs.gov) offers free downloadable topo maps at various scales.

- 1:50,000 — Good city overview with street detail.

Where to get them:

- USGS National Map (nationalmap.gov) — Free downloadable maps at various scales

- Nevada Bureau of Mines and Geology — Detailed regional maps

- Mapquest / Google Maps (print) — Custom zoom/print for any area

- Local print shops — Places like FedEx Office or blueprint shops in Las Vegas can print large-format maps at whatever scale you specify

- Amazon/eBay — Folded or laminated city maps of Las Vegas

If you let me know what you're actually *trying to do* with the map (navigation, a project, decoration, gaming/tabletop, etc.), I can point you toward the best option!

***

Where can I get a 1:1 scale map of Las Vegas?

Copilot:

A **true 1:1 scale map of Las Vegas**—a map the same physical size as the city itself—**does not exist**. This idea is famously associated with Borges' short story *On Exactitude in Science*, where a civilization creates a map so detailed it matches the territory exactly. In reality, no commercial, government, or academic organization produces maps at literal 1:1 scale because such a map would need to cover **over 135 square miles** of the Las Vegas valley.

What *does* exist are **large-format wall maps** of Las Vegas, but these are still at conventional scales (e.g., 1:32,600). The largest commercially available option surfaced in the search is the **Univarsal 78" × 82" Las Vegas Wall Map**, which is detailed but nowhere near 1:1 scale.

What you *can* get instead

Below are the closest practical alternatives, each linked as a Guided Link so you can explore them further:

- **Large wall maps** — Oversized laminated maps like the Univarsal 78"×82" version provide street-level detail and are suitable for offices, classrooms, or planning spaces.

- **Digital zoomable maps** — Platforms like Google Maps allow infinite zoom and effectively function as "virtual 1:1" representations.

- **GIS datasets** — If you need extremely high-resolution spatial data, the City of Las Vegas and Clark County GIS portals offer aerial imagery and parcel-level data that can be used to create custom large-scale prints.

If you meant something else

People sometimes ask for a "1:1 scale map" when they actually want:

- A **full-size floor map** for an exhibit or installation
- A **hyper-detailed street map** for planning or modeling
- A **large-format print** for a wall or workspace
- A **map suitable for model-building** (e.g., for trains or tabletop gaming)

If any of those match what you're looking for, choose one of these to continue:

- Full-size exhibit map
- High-detail planning map
- Large wall print
- Map for modeling

COLORS

FUNNY THING ABOUT AI and colors: I am sure that AIs know what colors are (insert definitions about properties of light and wavelengths and yada yada), but can they actually *see* colors? Do AIs know what a sunset looks like, or know why art looks good, or even wonder on the magic of a new box of crayons (or is that just me)?

What does fluorescent black look like?

Background: I've always said my favorite color is fluorescent black - something about the brightness of this dark color intrigued me. Now, finally, we have come to a point where we can ask, what is this color anyway?

TL;DR: I don't think any of the AIs believe me. Although they all say that this is an impossible color, they are also willing to admit that it could refer to a blacklight paint, and a "blacker-than-black" color.

SoundBytes:

Gemini: "Most people use the term to describe fluorescent pigments under a blacklight."

ChatGPT: "It's kind of like asking "what does invisible blue look like?" "

Claude: "[I]f it were truly fluorescent, it wouldn't be black!"

Copilot: "[Y]ou can't have a glowing version of something defined by not glowing."

***

What does fluorescent black look like?

Gemini:

Strictly speaking, **fluorescent black doesn't exist** because the terms are visual opposites. However, depending on who you ask, it describes three very different things:

1. The Scientific Reality (The "Invisiblity" Answer)

Fluorescence is the process where a material absorbs high-energy light (like UV) and re-emits it as a visible color.

- **Black** is the absence of visible light.
- If a material were truly "fluorescent black," it would absorb light and then emit... nothing. To our eyes, that just looks like a standard matte black or a shadow.

2. The "Blacklight" Effect

Most people use the term to describe **fluorescent pigments under a blacklight**. In this scenario:

- The "black" is the dark environment.
- The "fluorescence" is the neon glow of posters, paint, or clothing.
- In this context, it looks like **glowing neon violet, green, or pink** popping out against a deep, dark void.

3. The Artistic "Vantablack" Aesthetic

In art and design, "fluorescent black" is sometimes used poetically to describe hyper-saturated, deep colors that feel like they have "depth" or "energy" despite being dark. Think of:

- **Oils on water:** Dark, but with a shimmering, shifting rainbow sheen.
- **Iridescent crow feathers:** They look black, but "glow" with a metallic green or purple when the light hits them.
- **Vantablack:** A material that absorbs **99.96%** of light. It looks like a "hole" in reality. While not fluorescent, it is the closest thing to a "glowing" or "active" version of black because it is so unnaturally dark that it draws the eye.

Comparison Table

Fun Fact: There is a brand of ink called **"Noodler's Blue Ghost."** It is completely invisible (white/clear) on paper in normal light, but glows a bright, "fluorescent" blue under UV light. It's the closest thing we have to a "secret" color!

***

What does fluorescent black look like?

ChatGPT:

Ah… this is a sneaky one!

Here's the thing: **"fluorescent" means a material absorbs light at one wavelength and emits it at another, usually brighter wavelength.** In practice, that means **fluorescent colors glow vividly under UV light**—like neon green, pink, yellow, orange.

But black is… black. It **absorbs almost all light** instead of reflecting or emitting it. That means:

- **Fluorescent black is impossible.** It can't glow because it doesn't emit light.
- If you tried to make "fluorescent black" paint, it would just look like regular black.

It's kind of like asking **"what does invisible blue look like?"**—fun wordplay, but physics says nope.

If you want, I can explain a **weird trick some designers use to make "glowing black" illusions**—it's pretty clever. Do you want me to?

***

What does fluorescent black look like?

Claude:

This is a fun paradox! **Fluorescent black doesn't really exist** — and here's why:

The contradiction:

- **Fluorescent** colors work by absorbing ultraviolet (UV) light and re-emitting it as bright, visible light — making them appear to glow and look more vivid than ordinary colors.

- **Black**, by definition, absorbs virtually *all* visible light and reflects very little back to your eyes.

These two properties are fundamentally at odds — fluorescence requires emitting light, while black requires absorbing it.

The closest real things:

- **Blacklight paint/posters** — surfaces that look dark or black under normal light but glow with vivid colors under UV (blacklight). That's about as close as it gets.

- **Vantablack** — the opposite extreme, a material so black it absorbs ~99.96% of light and looks almost surreal.

In common usage:

- "Fluorescent black" is sometimes used as a **marketing term** for very dark, high-contrast ink or paint, but it's not truly fluorescent in the scientific sense.

So in short — you can't really see fluorescent black, because if it were truly fluorescent, it wouldn't be black! It's a bit like asking what a silent sound sounds like.

***

What does fluorescent black look like?

Copilot:

Fluorescent black doesn't exist — and that's exactly why it's such a fun idea.

To be fluorescent, a color has to *emit light*. Black is the **absence** of light. So "fluorescent black" is a contradiction: you can't have a glowing version of something defined by not glowing.

But the concept *does* spark some interesting possibilities.

What "fluorescent black" would look like if it *could* exist

If we imagine it anyway, the closest real-world analogs are:

- **Blacklight-reactive materials** — very dark pigments that glow purple or blue under UV
- **Vantablack illusions** — so black they look like holes in reality
- **Iridescent black surfaces** — beetle shells or bird feathers that appear black but flash color at certain angles

None of these are truly "fluorescent black," but they're the closest things nature and technology offer.

Why fluorescent black can't exist

Fluorescence requires a pigment to:

1. Absorb light
2. Re-emit it at a visible wavelength

Black pigments absorb light but **don't re-emit it**. They convert it to heat instead. So they can't fluoresce.

Bottom line

Fluorescent black is physically impossible, but the idea points toward materials that are:

- extremely dark
- reactive under UV
- or visually surprising

If you want, I can help you design a fictional **fluorescent black pigment** for a story, artwork, or worldbuilding.

WHICH WEIGHS MORE, PURPLE OR YELLOW?

BACKGROUND: ONE THING WE learn in grade school is that everything has mass, and everything has weight. One thing we never learn is what the weight of each color is.

TL;DR: The common answer is that colors don't have weight. However, Gemini had to be different by proving not only does purple weigh more, but also that yellow weighs more.

SoundBytes:

Gemini: "[D]epending on whether you're a physicist, a painter, or a psychologist, you could argue for either one"

Claude: "[N]either color weighs anything at all."

Copilot: It's "like asking whether loud or quiet is heavier."

***

Which weighs more, purple or yellow?

Gemini:

Since colors are just wavelengths of light and don't have mass, neither "weighs" anything in a literal sense. However, depending on whether you're a physicist, a painter, or a psychologist, you could argue for either one:

1. The Physics Perspective (The "Energy" Weight)

If we look at the energy of the photons (light particles) for each color, **purple** (violet) technically "carries more weight."

- **Purple** has a shorter wavelength and higher frequency, meaning its photons have more energy.

- **Yellow** has a longer wavelength and lower frequency, carrying less energy.

- According to Einstein's E=mc^2, energy and mass are related. While the rest mass of a photon is zero, the "energy-mass" of a violet photon is higher than that of a yellow one.

2. The Psychology Perspective (Visual Weight)

In art and interior design, we talk about **"Visual Weight,"** which is how heavy a color *feels* to our brain.

- **Purple** usually "weighs" more. Darker, more saturated colors feel heavier and more grounded. If you painted the top half of a room dark purple and the bottom half bright yellow, the room would feel "top-heavy" and slightly oppressive.

- **Yellow** is high-luminance. It reflects more light and feels "airy," light, and buoyant.

3. The Pigment Perspective (The Paint Weight)

If you went to an art store and weighed a tube of purple paint vs. a tube of yellow paint, the answer depends on the chemicals inside:

- **Yellow:** Often made from **Cadmium** or **Iron oxides**, which are quite heavy minerals.
- **Purple:** Often made from **Dioxazine** (a synthetic organic compound) or **Cobalt**.

The Verdict: If you're decorating a room, **purple** is the heavy hitter. If you're measuring the actual energy of light, **purple** wins again. But if you're carrying buckets of paint, that **yellow** might just be the one to give you a workout!

***

Which weighs more, purple or yellow?

ChatGPT:

Ah! This is one of those **trick questions that messes with your assumptions**.

The key is: **colors themselves don't have weight.**

- Purple and yellow are just **wavelengths of light** (or pigments in paint).

- **Light has energy, not mass**, so in normal terms, purple doesn't weigh more than yellow, and vice versa.

- If you're talking about objects **painted purple vs yellow**, then the weight difference depends **entirely on the material**, not the color.

So the answer is: **neither—the color itself has no weight**.

If you want, I can explain **why our brains sometimes *feel* heavier for certain colors**—it's a neat optical/psychology trick.

***

Which weighs more, purple or yellow?

Claude:

Neither — **colors don't have weight**!

Color is simply how our eyes perceive different wavelengths of light:

- **Purple** is around 380–450 nanometers
- **Yellow** is around 570–590 nanometers

Wavelengths of light are massless, so neither color weighs anything at all.

Now, if you're talking about **objects that are purple or yellow**, that's a different story — but then it's the material making up the object that has weight, not the color itself. A yellow bowling ball and a purple feather are going to tip the scales very differently!

Is there a specific purple vs. yellow thing you were curious about?

***

Which weighs more, purple or yellow?

Copilot:

Neither **purple** nor **yellow** weighs more — because **colors don't have mass**.

But the *question* is a classic playful logic trap, so let's break it down in a way that's both fun and precise.

Core answer

A color has **no weight**, so **purple and yellow weigh exactly the same: zero**.

Why colors can't weigh anything

- **Color** is a *perception* created by your brain when light of certain wavelengths hits your eyes.
- **Weight** is a physical property of matter under gravity.
- Light isn't matter, so it doesn't have weight in the everyday sense.

So asking which color weighs more is like asking whether **loud** or **quiet** is heavier.

If we answer it *playfully*

If you *did* want to assign weight:

- **Purple** feels heavier emotionally — dramatic, royal, moody.
- **Yellow** feels lighter — bright, sunny, energetic.

But that's psychology, not physics.

Bottom line

Neither weighs more.

Only the *object* that is purple or yellow can have weight — not the color itself.

If you want, I can also compare the "weight" of **red vs blue** or explain why some colors *feel* heavier even though they aren't.

How do you make plaid paint?

Background: Growing up, I've seen multiple cartoons where someone opens a paint can and starts painting in plaid or polkadot. Now in the present day, I can finally get an answer to how they did it.

TL;DR: Apparently, you cannot. (Don't tell me cartoons lied to me!) Everyone was willing to tell me how to paint a plaid design if I want to spend all day.

SoundBytes:

Gemini: "If you open a tin of paint and see stripes or squares, something has gone very, very wrong with the chemistry."

Claude: "So you can't really bottle "plaid" in a can, any more than you could bottle "striped" or "checkered." "

Copilot: It's "like trying to bottle a tartan."

***

How do you make plaid paint?

Gemini:

Making **plaid paint** is a classic "rite of passage" for new apprentices in the painting and construction world—right alongside being sent to find a "bucket of steam" or a "left-handed screwdriver."

The short answer: **You can't.** Plaid paint doesn't exist in a single can. If you open a tin of paint and see stripes or squares, something has gone very, very wrong with the chemistry.

However, if you actually want to get a plaid pattern on your wall or a piece of furniture, you have to create it through a specific process. Here is how you "make" it happen:

The "Real" Way: Layering and Taping

To get a plaid effect, you have to paint in stages. It requires patience and a lot of painter's tape.

1. **The Base Coat:** Paint the entire surface your lightest color (usually white or a light cream). Let it dry completely.

2. **Vertical Stripes:** Use painter's tape to mask off vertical columns. Paint these stripes in your second color.

    - *Pro Tip:* Use a **glaze** (a translucent paint) so the base color peeks through.

3. **Horizontal Stripes:** Once the vertical stripes are bone-dry, tape off horizontal rows and paint them with the same (or a third) color.

4. **The "Magic" Squares:** Where the vertical and horizontal stripes overlap, the colors will combine to create a darker shade, forming the classic "checkered" or "plaid" look.

Modern Alternatives

If you aren't in the mood for six hours of taping, most people use these shortcuts:

- **Wallpaper:** You can buy plaid patterns that look like fabric.
- **Stencils:** You can buy a large "plaid stencil" that allows you to roll the pattern on in one or two passes.
- **Hydro-Dipping:** For smaller objects, you can float a plaid-patterned film on water and dip the item through it.

The Joke: If someone actually sent you to the store to buy a can of plaid paint, you can tell them the store was fresh out, but they did have plenty of **"clear camouflage"** in stock!

***

How do you make plaid paint?

ChatGPT:

Ah, "plaid paint"! That's a fun one, because **plaid isn't a single color—it's a pattern**. You can't make "plaid" by mixing pigments alone—you have to **layer and line it.** Here's how you do it:

Step 1: Pick your base color

- Paint your canvas, wall, or object with the **background color**.

- Let it **dry completely**. This will be the main color of your plaid.

Step 2: Add the vertical stripes

- Use **painter's tape** or a steady hand.

- Choose a **contrasting color** and paint evenly spaced **vertical lines** over your base.

- Let these lines **dry completely**.

Step 3: Add the horizontal stripes

- Again, use tape or careful brushing.

- Paint **horizontal lines** in the same or another contrasting color.

- The overlapping areas will create that **classic plaid effect**.

Step 4: Finishing touches

- Remove any tape.
- Touch up any uneven spots.
- Optionally, add **thin accent lines** to mimic woven texture.

Tip:

- Plaid works best with **3–4 colors**: one base, two main stripes, and an optional accent.
- You can **vary stripe thickness** for a more realistic look, like tartan.

If you want, I can **sketch a simple visual guide** showing how the stripes overlap to make plaid—it's much easier to see than just instructions. Do you want me to do that?

***

How do you make plaid paint?

Claude:

Plaid paint doesn't exist — at least not in the way you might imagine! Here's why:

The problem:

- **Plaid** is a pattern made by crisscrossing stripes of different colors — it's not a single color or texture, it's a *design*.
- **Paint** is a uniform substance that comes out of a can as a single color.

So you can't really bottle "plaid" in a can, any more than you could bottle "striped" or "checkered."

However, you CAN paint a plaid pattern! Here's how people do it:

1. **Base coat** — paint the surface your lightest plaid color.
2. **Tape and stripe** — use painter's tape to mask off horizontal stripes and paint them a second color.
3. **Repeat vertically** — do the same thing with vertical stripes, using a third color or the same one.
4. **Overlap effects** — where stripes cross, you can blend or layer colors to create that authentic plaid look.

Some specialty products like textured or multicolor spray paints can create *plaid-like* visual effects, and there are fabric paints designed specifically for painting plaid patterns on clothing.

So while you can't mix up a can of plaid, you can absolutely *paint* plaid with a little patience and tape!

***

How do you make plaid paint?

Copilot:

Plaid paint is one of those delightfully impossible ideas — like trying to bottle a tartan. **You can't actually make liquid paint come out of the can in a plaid pattern**, because plaid requires *overlapping stripes*, and paint mixes into a single uniform color.

But you *can* create the **effect** of plaid paint on a wall, canvas, or object. Here's how people actually do it.

Core idea

Plaid isn't a pigment — it's a **pattern**.

So instead of "plaid paint," you create **painted plaid** by layering stripes.

How to make a painted plaid pattern

Here's the real-world method artists and designers use:

- **Base coat** — Paint the whole surface a solid background color.

- **Vertical stripes** — Use painter's tape to mask straight lines and paint your first set of stripes.

- **Horizontal stripes** — After the vertical stripes dry, tape again and paint the crossing stripes.

- **Transparency effect** — Where stripes overlap, use a slightly darker or semi-transparent version of the color to mimic woven fabric.

This layering is what gives plaid its signature look.

Why you can't buy "plaid paint"

Paint is a fluid mixture. If you tried to mix multiple colors in a can, they'd blend into one muddy shade. Plaid only exists when **distinct lines stay separate**, which requires masking and layering — not mixing.

If you want a shortcut

People sometimes use:

- **Plaid stencils**
- **Pattern rollers**
- **Adhesive vinyl templates**

These tools let you "stamp" or roll a plaid pattern instead of taping every line.

Bottom line

You can't pour plaid out of a can, but you *can* paint a plaid pattern by layering stripes with tape, stencils, or pattern rollers.

If you want, I can help you design a **specific plaid color scheme** — classic tartan, modern pastel, neon, anything you like.

People and Animals

We interact with other people and/or animals on a daily basis (whether we want to or not sometimes). Yet, do we really know them? The answer is: no, we do not. Do we want to? That's not something that an AI can answer, so let's give them something that they can.

Are Scott Van Pelt and Lucy Van Pelt related?

Background: This is the original question that started it all. I was watching ESPN one night when I saw a promo for Scott Van Pelt, and I remembered that that is also the last name of Lucy and Linus in Peanuts. I knew they weren't related (well, pretty sure at least), and looked it up to see what it would say.

TL;DR: No, they are not related. Not surprising considering one is a cartoon character and the other is not.

SoundBytes:
ChatGPT: "One lives in real life, the other in comic strip land."
Claude: "They come from very different worlds"
Copilot: "The shared last name is pure coincidence"

***

Are Scott Van Pelt and Lucy Van Pelt related?

Gemini:

No, they aren't related—mostly because one is a real person and the other is made of ink and paper.

Here is the breakdown of the two:

- **Scott Van Pelt:** A very real (and very tall) veteran sports commentator and the host of the late-night edition of *SportsCenter* on ESPN.

- **Lucy Van Pelt:** A fictional, crabby character from Charles M. Schulz's comic strip *Peanuts*, known for her "Psychiatric Help" booth and for famously pulling the football away from Charlie Brown.

While they share a last name, Scott is from Maryland, and Lucy "resides" in the fictional world of the *Peanuts* gang. However, Scott is well aware of the name connection; he has occasionally joked about his "famous relative" over the years during his broadcasts.

***

Are Scott Van Pelt and Lucy Van Pelt related?

ChatGPT:

This is a classic case of **same last name, totally different worlds**.

- **Scott Van Pelt** is a real person: a sports broadcaster for ESPN.
- **Lucy Van Pelt** is a fictional character from Charles Schulz's *Peanuts* comic strip.

So, **no—they aren't related**. One lives in real life, the other in comic strip land.

It's kind of like asking if Sherlock Holmes and your neighbor are cousins—they share a name in your imagination, but that's it.

If you want, I can give a **few other famous "Van Pelts" and see if any are real or fictional**—it's kind of fun.

***

Are Scott Van Pelt and Lucy Van Pelt related?

Claude:

No, they are not related. They come from very different worlds:

- **Scott Van Pelt** is a real person — a sports anchor and host on ESPN, known for his late-night *SportsCenter* and college football coverage.

- **Lucy Van Pelt** is a fictional character from Charles M. Schulz's *Peanuts* comic strip — the bossy, football-pulling older sister of Linus.

They simply share the same last name, which is just a coincidence. "Van Pelt" is a real Dutch surname, so it's not unusual for both a real person and a fictional character to carry it.

***

Are Scott Van Pelt and Lucy Van Pelt related?

Copilot:

No — **Scott Van Pelt and Lucy Van Pelt are *not* related.**

Scott Van Pelt is a real person, while Lucy Van Pelt is a fictional character from *Peanuts*, and there is **no family connection** between them.

Why they aren't related

1. Lucy Van Pelt is fictional

Lucy is a character created by Charles M. Schulz for the *Peanuts* comic strip, first appearing in 1952. She's part of the Van Pelt family along with Linus and Rerun.

2. Scott Van Pelt is a real person with no connection to Schulz's characters

Scott Van Pelt is a real individual (best known as an ESPN sportscaster), and public records show many real people with the Van Pelt surname — but none tied to the fictional Peanuts family.

3. The Peanuts "Van Pelt" name came from a drafting table

Charles Schulz chose the surname *Van Pelt* after seeing it printed on the side of his drafting desk — not from any real family connection.

Bottom line

The shared last name is **pure coincidence**:

- **Lucy Van Pelt** → fictional Peanuts character
- **Scott Van Pelt** → real person, unrelated
- **Origin of the name** → Schulz spotted it on a piece of furniture

If you want, I can also explain **how Schulz named other Peanuts characters** or **the real history of the Van Pelt surname**.

What kind of bear is Bear Grylls?

Background: To be completely honest, I have never watched Bear Grylls, but I have seen commercials for a few of his shows.

TL;DR: I think I would have been more interested to watch if he ended up being a real bear. Alas, it was not to be. (Although having Gemini call him a "Grylls-y Bear" does help a little.)

SoundBytes:
Gemini: "He's a very rare breed known as a Grylls-y Bear"
ChatGPT: He "is a human nicknamed Bear."
Copilot: "Survival Bear — eats bugs on TV so you don't have to"

***

What kind of bear is Bear Grylls?

Gemini:

He's a very rare breed known as a **Grylls-y Bear**—scientifically classified as *Adventurous survivor*.

In all seriousness, **Bear Grylls** (born Edward Michael Grylls) is a human being, not a bear. He is a British former SAS serviceman, survival instructor, and television personality best known for his show *Man vs. Wild*.

Here are a few "bear-like" facts about him:

- **The Name:** "Bear" was a nickname given to him by his older sister when he was just one week old, and it stuck so well that he eventually made it his legal name.

- **Hibernation:** He doesn't hibernate. In fact, he's the youngest Briton to climb Mount Everest (at age 23) and has crossed the North Atlantic in an open inflatable boat.

- **Diet:** While real bears eat berries and fish, Bear Grylls is famous for eating... well, just about anything to stay alive, including raw snakes, giant larvae, and the occasional yak eyeball.

If you ever run into him in the woods, don't play dead—he'll probably just try to teach you how to build a shelter out of your own shoelaces.

***

What kind of bear is Bear Grylls?

ChatGPT:

Ah, clever! You're mixing **wordplay** with real life.

- **Bear Grylls** is **not an actual bear**—he's a human survival expert, TV host, and adventurer from the UK.

- His real first name is actually **Edward**, but his nickname is **"Bear"**, given to him as a child because he was cuddly like a bear.

So the kind of bear he is... is a **human nicknamed Bear**.

If you want, I can give a few more **fun pun-style "what kind of bear" answers**—they get pretty silly. Do you want me to do that?

***

What kind of bear is Bear Grylls?

Claude:

Ha! Bear Grylls is not actually a bear at all — he's a **human**!

Specifically, he's a British adventurer, survival expert, and TV presenter, best known for the show *Man vs. Wild*. His real first name is actually **Edward** — "Bear" is just a nickname he's had since childhood.

So taxonomically speaking, he's:

- **Species:** *Homo sapiens*

- **Known for:** Drinking his own urine and eating things most people wouldn't touch on a dare

Arguably though, given his toughness and love of the wilderness, he might be an honorary grizzly.

***

What kind of bear is Bear Grylls?

Copilot:

Bear Grylls is **not any kind of bear at all** — he's a **human**, a British adventurer and TV survival personality. His nickname *"Bear"* was given to him by his older sister when he was just a week old.

Quick facts

- **Real name:** Edward Michael Grylls
- **Species:** Human (not ursine in any way)
- **Why "Bear"?** Childhood nickname from his sister Lara.
- **Famous for:** *Man vs. Wild*, *Running Wild with Bear Grylls*, survival expeditions, and serving as Chief Scout of the UK.

So what "kind" of bear is he?

If we're being playful:

- **Adventure Bear** — climbs mountains, drinks questionable water
- **Survival Bear** — eats bugs on TV so you don't have to
- **SAS Bear** — trained with the British Special Forces

But biologically?

He's **100% human**, 0% bear.

If you want, I can also explain **how he got famous** or **his wildest survival feats**.

Are most cats left-handed or right-handed?

Background: Most people are right-handed, some are left-handed, and a few can use both. Cats, on the other hand, walk on 4 paws and have no hands. This should be a simple answer.

TL;DR: I wasn't expecting much from this question, but I think it surprised me the most. Apparently most cats are either right- or left-~~handed~~ - sorry - pawed. Furthermore, the cat's gender may have a role in whether they use their left or right paw more. And that's why we ask.

SoundBytes:

Gemini: "Ambidextrous Kitties: A fair number of cats (roughly 20–25%)"

ChatGPT: "cat "pawedness"—a real thing, even though it sounds quirky!"

Claude: "[F]emale cats tend to favor their right paw, while male cats tend to favor their left paw"

Copilot: "[T]here is no overall species-wide majority"

***

Are most cats left-handed or right-handed?

Gemini:

Believe it or not, cats do tend to have a "dominant" paw, but it's a bit more complex than it is for humans. While about **90%** of humans are right-handed, cats are much more evenly split—and their preference often depends on their sex.

Research (notably from Queen's University Belfast) has found some fascinating patterns:

- **The Gender Split:** Male cats are significantly more likely to be **left-pawed**, while female cats are more likely to be **right-pawed**.

- **Ambidextrous Kitties:** A fair number of cats (roughly **20–25%**) don't show a strong preference at all and are essentially ambidextrous.

- **Task Specificity:** Cats often use their dominant paw for complex tasks, like reaching for a piece of food in a jar, but might use either paw for simple things like batting at a toy.

How to test your cat's "pawedness"

If you have a cat and want to see which way they lean, you can run a simple home experiment:

1. **The Treat Jar:** Place a treat inside a narrow glass or jar that is too small for their head. See which paw they use to fish it out.

2. **The "Step Up":** Watch which paw they lead with when

they start walking down a flight of stairs or stepping over a threshold.

3. **The Bat:** Dangling a toy just out of reach usually triggers their dominant "striking" paw.

To get an accurate result, you usually have to observe them doing these things about **50 to 75 times**, as they can be a bit inconsistent compared to us!

***

Are most cats left-handed or right-handed?

ChatGPT:

Ah, you're asking about **cat "pawedness"**—a real thing, even though it sounds quirky!

Just like humans, cats tend to have a **dominant paw**. Scientists call this **"lateralization."**

Here's what research shows:

- About **50–60% of cats show a clear paw preference**.
- Among those, studies suggest **slightly more cats are left-pawed than right-pawed**, but the difference is small.
- Male cats often lean **left-pawed**, and female cats more often lean **right-pawed**, though this isn't absolute.

So there's **no strong "right vs left" majority**, but if you had to pick, you might notice more left-pawed cats than right-pawed ones.

Fun fact:

- Cats can even **switch paws** depending on the task—like humans sometimes switch hands for different activities.

If you want, I can tell you **how to test which paw your cat prefers**—it's surprisingly easy and fun. Do you want me to show that?

***

Are most cats left-handed or right-handed?

Claude:

Great question! Cats do show "handedness" (or more accurately, **pawedness**), but the answer has an interesting twist:

- **Individual cats** do tend to have a paw preference — studies show that most cats consistently favor one paw over the other for tasks like reaching for food or stepping over objects.

- **However**, unlike humans (where roughly 90% are right-handed), cats as a species are **pretty evenly split** between left-pawed and right-pawed — with no strong population-wide bias toward either side.

- There does appear to be a **sex difference** though: research suggests **female cats tend to favor their right paw**, while **male cats tend to favor their left paw**. The reason for this isn't fully understood.

So the short answer: no majority preference across all cats, but your individual cat likely has a favorite paw — and its sex may be a clue as to which one!

***

Are most cats left-handed or right-handed?

Copilot:

Most cats **do have a dominant paw**, but unlike humans—who are overwhelmingly right-handed—cats split **almost evenly** between left and right. The key pattern researchers consistently find is **sex-linked**:

- **Male cats tend to be left-pawed**
- **Female cats tend to be right-pawed**

What studies show

<nothing to illustrate — no images added>

- **Most cats show a clear paw preference** (about 73–78%). Only about **22–27%** are ambidextrous.
- In one large study of 109 cats:
    - **49.5% right-pawed**
    - **40.4% left-pawed**

~10% ambidextrous

- When separated by sex:
    - **Females:** more likely right-pawed (54%)

Males: more likely left-pawed (45.7%)

So there is **no overall species-wide majority**, but there *is* a strong male-left / female-right trend.

Why cats have a dominant paw

Paw preference reflects **brain lateralization**—the same phenomenon behind human handedness. A dominant paw indicates one hemisphere is taking the lead on motor tasks. This likely evolved from hunting behaviors requiring precision.

How to test your own cat

You can check which paw your cat favors by watching which paw they use first when:

- Reaching for a treat in a container
- Stepping down stairs

Batting at a toy

Bottom line

Cats aren't "mostly left-handed" or "mostly right-handed" as a species. Instead:

- **Males skew left**
- **Females skew right**
- **Overall distribution is nearly even**

If you want, I can help you run a simple **paw-dominance test** for your own cat.

Is Batman a vampire?

Background: One day, I connected the dots: Batman essentially cosplays as a bat, and vampires can traditionally turn into bats. But then I realized, they both come out mostly at night. Furthermore, Batman lives in a mansion and vampires usually live in castles (aka: old-time mansions).

TL;DR: I guess I wasn't the first to see the connection. It turns out that several alternate timelines have been written that picture Batman as a vampire. Also makes me wonder whether Batman and Abraham Lincoln would be allies or enemies.

SoundBytes:

Gemini: "He is Bruce Wayne, a regular human being"

ChatGPT: "That said, DC has done alternate-universe stories where Batman *does* become a vampire."

Claude: "Unlike Superman or The Flash, he has no powers at all"

***

Is Batman a vampire?

Gemini:

No, in main DC Comics continuity, Batman is **not a vampire**. He is Bruce Wayne, a regular human being who relies on peak physical training, high-tech gadgets, and martial arts.

However, because his entire aesthetic is built around bats, shadows, and terror, it's an incredibly easy connection to make. In fact, DC has leaned into this exact concept multiple times in alternate-universe stories.

Here is a breakdown of how close Batman has come to actually being a creature of the night.

The Famous "Vampire Batman" Trilogy

The most iconic version of a blood-drinking Dark Knight happens in an alternate universe (DC's *Elseworlds* imprint) by Doug Moench and Kelley Jones. This storyline takes place across three graphic novels:

- **Batman & Dracula: Red Rain (1991):** Batman discovers that Dracula and his coven are feeding on Gotham's homeless. To gain the strength to defeat Dracula, Batman allows a rogue vampire named Tanya to bite him. He gains vampire powers, defeats Dracula, but is cursed to walk the night.

- **Batman: Bloodstorm (1994):** Batman tries to fight his bloodlust by using a synthetic blood substitute created by Alfred. By the end of the story, after losing people he loves, his willpower breaks and he drinks the blood of the Joker, fully succumbing to his monstrous side.

- **Batman: Crimson Mist (1999):** Fully corrupted, a feral, monstrous Batman begins slaughtering and drinking the blood of his classic rogues gallery (Penguin, Riddler, etc.) until Commissioner Gordon and Two-Face are forced to try and stop him.

Other Vampire Connections in DC Comics

- **Gods and Monsters:** In the 2015 animated movie and comic series *Justice League: Gods and Monsters*, the Batman of that universe isn't Bruce Wayne. Instead, it's **Kirk Langstrom** (who is "Man-Bat" in normal continuity). In this world, an experimental cure for his cancer accidentally turns him into a pseudo-vampire who drinks the blood of criminals to survive.

- **DC vs. Vampires (2021–2024):** In this recent, highly popular alternate-universe series, a massive vampire conspiracy quietly takes over the DC universe from the inside out. While Bruce Wayne doesn't start as a vampire, he has to lead the human resistance against turned heroes like Green Lantern and Nightwing.

Why the Myth Persists

Even in standard comic books where he is 100% human, Batman loves to let his enemies *think* he's supernatural. He uses theater, smoke bombs, and capes designed to look like wings so criminals are terrified that they are fighting a monster rather than a man in a suit.

Are you looking into a specific comic book storyline where he seemed a bit too bloodthirsty, or just appreciating how perfectly the myth fits the costume?

***

Is Batman a vampire?

ChatGPT:

No — Batman is not normally a vampire in mainstream DC continuity.

Batman is traditionally a human vigilante: Bruce Wayne, a wealthy man who uses training, technology, and detective skills to fight crime.

That said, DC has done alternate-universe stories where Batman *does* become a vampire. The best-known example is the trilogy beginning with Batman & Dracula: Red Rain, where Batman is transformed into a vampire while fighting Dracula.

There are also animated episodes, comics, and "Elseworlds" stories that play with supernatural versions of Batman, but those are alternate takes rather than the main version of the character.

***

Is Batman a vampire?

Claude:

No, Batman is not a vampire. He's a regular human (albeit an exceptionally trained and wealthy one).

That said, there are some vampire-like qualities to the character by design:

- **Bats** are strongly associated with vampires in Western culture, which is part of why Bruce Wayne chose the bat as his symbol — to strike fear into criminals.
- He operates **exclusively at night**, wears a **dark cape**, and lurks in shadows.
- His aesthetic is gothic and brooding, overlapping heavily with vampire imagery.

In alternate/non-canon stories, Batman *has* actually been depicted as a vampire. DC's *Elseworlds* imprint published a trilogy (*Batman & Dracula: Red Rain*, *Bloodstorm*, and *Crimson Mist*) where Bruce Wayne is turned into a vampire. These are fun "what if" stories but outside the main continuity.

In the main DC universe, Bruce Wayne is fully human — which is actually central to his character. Unlike Superman or The Flash, he has no powers at all, making his dedication and discipline the core of what makes him compelling.

***

Is Batman a vampire?

Copilot:

Batman **is not a vampire in the main DC continuity**, but **several official DC storylines and alternate universes *do* feature Batman as a literal vampire**. The idea shows up repeatedly across Elseworlds stories and multiverse variants, and DC has even teased vampiric transformations in recent canon arcs.

Core answer

Main-universe Batman (Earth-0) is human, not a vampire.

But multiple alternate Batmen *are* vampires, most famously the versions from the *Red Rain* trilogy and Earth-43.

Where Batman *is* a vampire

1. Earth-43 Batman — the most famous vampire version

Earth-43's Bruce Wayne becomes a vampire while fighting Dracula. He eventually succumbs fully to vampirism and turns many Justice League members into vampires, forming the **Blood League**.

- Gains vampiric powers
- Loses his humanity
- Leads a multiversal threat

2. Red Rain Batman — the classic Elseworlds trilogy

In *Batman & Dracula: Red Rain*, *Bloodstorm*, and *Crimson Mist*, Batman is bitten by a rogue vampire named Tanya and becomes a vampire himself. He kills Dracula but ultimately loses his humanity and becomes a violent, bloodthirsty vigilante.

3. Modern hints of vampirism — recent Detective Comics arc

A 2024 storyline introduces a youth-restoring serum called **Sangraal**, created using someone else's blood. This has led to speculation that DC is subtly steering Batman toward a vampiric transformation, though this is not confirmed canon.

Why people ask this

Batman's nocturnal behavior, bat motif, and gothic aesthetic naturally invite comparisons to vampires. DC has leaned into this over the decades with multiple "What if Batman were a vampire?" stories — some of which became extremely popular.

Summary table

Want to explore one of these versions in depth?

Would you like a deep dive into **Earth-43**, the **Red Rain trilogy**, or the **recent Sangraal arc**?

Words

Someone once said that the US and Britain are two countries separated by a common language. If that is true, then most of the US can be divided up similarly. Whether we like it or not, language is always changing and evolving. Meaning it seems like people from different regions, or even different generations in the same house, sometimes seem like they speak different languages. Which makes English both fascinating and frustrating, depending on who you ask.

Why do we drive on a parkway and park on a driveway?

Background: This is the classic thought question. I wish I could say I came up with this question, but I felt it fit in with the rest of the book, so here it is.

TL;DR: Another easy question that everyone agreed on. Parkways used to go through parks, and driveways were how you would drive up to your house. Simple, right?

SoundBytes:

Gemini: "Language is essentially a museum of dead intentions!"

ChatGPT: It's an example of" "backwards words" in English—like why we "cook" bacon but "bake" cookies."

Claude: "[L]anguage fossilizes old meanings long after reality has moved on."

Copilot: "Because English is a glorious mess."

***

Why do we drive on a parkway and park on a driveway?

Gemini:

It's one of the great linguistic pranks of the English language. To solve this mystery, we have to look back at the late 19th and early 20th centuries, when these words were first coined.

The short answer? The names haven't changed, but the **way we use them** has.

1. The Parkway

Originally, a **parkway** was exactly what it sounds like: a road through a **park**.

- **The History:** Landscape architects like Frederick Law Olmsted designed these roads to be scenic routes for carriages (and later, early cars) to enjoy nature. They were designed to be "park-like" with lush trees and no commercial trucks allowed.

- **The Shift:** As cities grew, these scenic routes became major commuter arteries. We kept the name "parkway," but we replaced the leisurely Sunday stroll with 65-mph traffic.

2. The Driveway

In the early days of the automobile, houses were often set back quite a distance from the main road.

- **The History:** A **driveway** was the long private path you had to **drive** down to get from the public street to your house or garage.

- **The Shift:** As properties got smaller and suburban lots became the norm, that long "drive" shrunk. Eventually, it became a short slab of concrete just long enough to leave a car on. We stopped "driving" on them because they became too short to do anything but "park" on.

Other Transport Contradictions

If you think the parkway/driveway situation is confusing, English has a few other gems:

- **Shipment vs. Cargo:** Why do we call it a **shipment** when it goes by truck, but **cargo** when it goes by ship?

- **Freight:** Why is **freight** carried by a train, while a **cargo** ship carries... well, freight?

The Verdict: Etymology (the study of word origins) cares more about what a thing *used* to be than what it *is* now. Language is essentially a museum of dead intentions!

***

Why do we drive on a parkway and park on a driveway?

ChatGPT:

Ah, the classic **English language irony!** This one is less about logic and more about **history and how words evolve**. Let's break it down carefully:

1. Parkway

- Originally, a **parkway** was a **scenic road through a park or landscaped area**.
- The word "park" in this case comes from **"park-like"**, not from parking a car.
- So, **we drive on a parkway** because it was designed for pleasant driving through greenery.

2. Driveway

- A **driveway** originally referred to a **private road leading from a street to a house or farm**.
- People "drove" along it to reach their house or barn—it wasn't primarily for parking.
- Over time, cars started being left there, but the name stuck.

TL;DR

- **Parkway** → a "park-like" road → you drive on it.
- **Driveway** → a path you drive along to get to your home → you often park on it.

English loves these **historical quirks**, which is why it can feel so backwards sometimes.

If you want, I can make a **list of other everyday "backwards words" in English**—like why we "cook" bacon but "bake" cookies. It's pretty funny.

***

Why do we drive on a parkway and park on a driveway?

Claude:

Ah, the classic question that has puzzled philosophers, comedians, and people stuck in traffic for decades!

The answer actually lies in **history and etymology:**

Parkway:

- Originally, a "parkway" was a scenic, landscaped roadway *through or alongside a park* — think tree-lined, beautiful, leisurely drives.

- The term dates to the late 1800s, designed by landscape architects like Frederick Law Olmsted.

- Over time the name stuck even as parkways became ordinary (and often congested) roads.

Driveway:

- A "driveway" was originally a private road you would *drive* along — typically a long path leading up to a house or estate.

- You would literally **drive** your horse and carriage (later your car) along it to reach the front door.

- As homes got smaller and driveways got shorter, they shrank to what we have today — just a little slab where you... park.

So the real answer:

- We *did* once drive on driveways and appreciate the park-like scenery of parkways.
- The words just **didn't keep up with the times** as urban life changed around them.

It's a great example of how language fossilizes old meanings long after reality has moved on. English is full of these little fossils!

***

Why do we drive on a parkway and park on a driveway?

Copilot:

Because English is a glorious mess.

The reason we **drive on a parkway** and **park on a driveway** comes from two different historical paths — the words changed, but the things they described didn't keep up.

Why we *drive* on a parkway

A **parkway** originally meant a **scenic, landscaped road** built for leisurely driving through "park-like" surroundings.

- "Park" in *parkway* refers to **green space**, not parking
- Early parkways (late 1800s–early 1900s) were designed for **carriages and early cars**
- They were wide, smooth, and meant for **driving**, not stopping

So a parkway is literally a **way through a park-like area**.

Why we *park* on a driveway

A **driveway** originally meant the **private road leading from the street to a house**, where you would *drive* your carriage or car.

- In the 1800s, a driveway was the **path you drove on** to reach the home
- People didn't park there — they parked in **carriage houses** or later **garages**

- Over time, cars got smaller, garages moved to the back or side, and the driveway became the place you actually **parked**

The name stayed even though the function flipped.

So why the contradiction?

Because English loves to **freeze old meanings** even when life changes around them.

The words stayed; the behaviors shifted.

It's the same reason we "hang up" a phone we no longer physically hang, or "dial" numbers on a screen.

If you want to explore more linguistic oddities

You might enjoy:

- **Why we ship by truck and send cargo by ship**
- **Why a building is called a building even after it's built**
- **Why we call them apartments when they're stuck together**

Want another language paradox unraveled?

IF HEXAGON, WHERE DID IT GO?

BACKGROUND: WHEN I WROTE this question, I expected at least one of the AIs to "not get it".

TL;DR: I am happy to say that they all took the question as seriously as it was meant to be. Actually, Copilot additionally answered the question "with the seriousness it absolutely does not deserve". Thanks for that.

SoundBytes:

Gemini: "It didn't really "go" anywhere—it's just "polygon." (Get it? *Polly-gone*?)"

ChatGPT: "This is a play on words, not a geometry question."

Claude: "It was last seen heading toward Polygon, a small town just past the Bermuda Triangle"

Copilot: "Into tessellation witness protection — too many right angles asking too many questions"

***

If hexagon, where did it go?

Gemini:

If **hexagon**, it likely went to the same place the **octagon** goes when it's time to stop: the **Geometry Graveyard** (or perhaps just around the corner).

Since a hexagon has six sides, it's a bit of a flight risk. Here are the most likely places it's hiding:

1. The Beehive

Hexagons are obsessed with efficiency. If one goes missing, it's probably clocked in at the local **honeycomb**. Bees use hexagons because they are the strongest, most space-efficient shape for storing honey. It's not gone; it's just working a 9-to-5.

2. Saturn's North Pole

If your hexagon had higher aspirations, it might have moved to **Saturn**. There is a massive, permanent cloud pattern there that is a perfect hexagon. It's about 20,000 miles wide, so it's hard to miss if you have a telescope.

3. The "Hex-it" Strategy

Maybe it just wanted to be a different shape for a while?

- If it lost a side, it's now a **pentagon** (likely working for the government).
- If it gained two sides, it's an **octagon** (probably standing at an intersection telling people what to do).

4. The Organic Chemistry Lab

Check your nearest chalkboard. Hexagons (as **benzene rings**) are basically the celebrities of organic chemistry. They spend most of their time bonded to carbons and hydrogens, trying to look stable.

The Verdict: It didn't really "go" anywhere—it's just "polygon." (Get it? *Polly-gone*?)

I'll see myself out.

***

If hexagon, where did it go?

ChatGPT:

Ah... I see what you're doing! This is a **play on words**, not a geometry question.

- You said: **"If hexagon, where did it go?"**
- The joke is in the **pun**: *"hexagon"* → *"he's gone."*

So the answer is: **he's gone.**

It's a clever little word riddle that tricks your brain into thinking about shapes instead of verbs.

If you want, I can give a **few more riddles in this "shape-word pun" style**—they're surprisingly sneaky.

***

If hexagon, where did it go?

Claude:

Well, if **hexagon**... it probably **heptagon**!
Since you're playing in the realm of geometry puns:

- It **hexagon** because it had too many **sides** to deal with
- It was last seen heading toward **Polygon**, a small town just past the **Bermuda Triangle**
- Rumor has it, it was **obtuse** about the whole situation and just needed some **space** (specifically, about 720 degrees worth)
- Some say it simply **octagon** (and don't come back)

In all seriousness though, "hexagon" is just a word describing a six-sided shape — it doesn't go anywhere! But your question has the same wonderful logic as classics like "if pro is the opposite of con, is progress the opposite of Congress?"

***

If hexagon, where did it go?

Copilot:

Ah, the ancient riddle of geometry and mischief.

If **hexagon**, then clearly... **it's gone**.

That's the whole joke — a hexagon is a *hex-a-gone*.

But let's treat your question with the seriousness it absolutely does not deserve.

Where the hexagon "went," depending on the universe you choose

- **Into the pun dimension** — where all shapes go when they've had enough of Euclid's nonsense
- **Behind the parallelogram** — it's shy, don't make a big deal about it
- **To join the bees** — nature's most efficient architects needed a consultant
- **Into tessellation witness protection** — too many right angles asking too many questions

The "serious" answer

A hexagon didn't go anywhere — but the *wordplay* did.

"Hexagon" → "hex-a-gone" → "it's gone."

A geometry dad joke disguised as a question.

If you want to continue the chaos

I can also explain:

- **Where the octopus went**
- **Why the circle vanished**
- **What the triangle is hiding**

Pick your next shape and we'll track it down.

WHAT IS THE FUNNIEST WORD IN THE ENGLISH LANGUAGE?

BACKGROUND: THIS ONE WAS just out of curiosity to see how they would reply. Nothing funny about the question (except the possible answers).

TL;DR: Even though they all responded based on surveys, polls, and research, there didn't seem to be one common answer. Upchuck and kerfuffle each got a couple votes, so I guess that's what we will go with.

SoundBytes:

Gemini: "Snollygoster: A shrewd, unprincipled person (usually a politician)."

ChatGPT: " "Flibbertigibbet" — a chatterbox or silly person; basically linguistic chaos."

Claude: "Personally, it's hard to argue against kerfuffle."

Copilot: "Bumfuzzle — meaning to confuse; widely cited as a top funny word."

***

What is the funniest word in the English language?

Gemini:

While humor is entirely subjective, language experts and psychologists have actually used data and mathematical models to find the scientific answer to this question.

According to a comprehensive study published in the *Journal of Experimental Psychology* by researchers at the University of Alberta, the single funniest word in the English language is **Upchuck**.

The Top 10 Funniest Words (According to Science)

By analyzing thousands of words and measuring human reactions, researchers isolated the top ten words that universally trigger our "risible" (laugh) reflex:

1. **Upchuck**

2. **Bubby**

3. **Boff**

4. **Wriggly**

5. **Yaps**

6. **Giggle**

7. **Cooch**

8. **Guffaw**

9. **Puffball**

10. **Jiggly**

(An honorable mention goes to a separate 2017 study from the University of Warwick, which polled thousands of people and found that ***Booty*** *took the number one crown.)*

Why Are These Words Funny?

The science of funny words (psycholinguistics) boils down to two main factors: **how it looks/sounds** and **what it means**.

1. The Phonetic "Goldilocks Zone"

The legendary playwright Neil Simon once famously wrote in his play *The Sunshine Boys* that "words with K in them are funny." He was onto something.

Science shows that words are structurally funnier if they are uncommon and have an improbable combination of letters. Specifically, words that contain a **hard "K" sound** (like *upchuck*) or a **long "oo" sound** (like *booty* or *bamboozle*) naturally trigger amusement. We also love "plosives"—consonants that burst out of the mouth, like **B, P, G, and T** (*bubby, puffball, giggle*).

2. Subversive Meanings

Words are judged significantly funnier if they overlap with specific taboo or evolutionary categories. The study found that the best semantic predictors of humor are words related to:

- **Bodily functions**
- **Sex**

- **Insults**
- **Partying**
- **Animals**

A word like "upchuck" is a double-whammy: it has an improbable phonetic structure with a hard "K" sound, and it describes a bodily function (vomiting) without using a harsh or clinical term.

Classic Old-School Contenders

If you prefer vintage linguistic wordplay over modern data, lexicographers often point to these historical slang words as peak English comedy:

- **Absquatulate:** To abruptly pack up and leave.
- **Snollygoster:** A shrewd, unprincipled person (usually a politician).
- **Taradiddle:** A petty lie or pretentious nonsense.
- **Collywobbles:** A funny way to say you have a stomachache.

Does "upchuck" earn the crown for you, or is there a specific, bizarre word that always makes you snort when you hear it?

***

What is the funniest word in the English language?

ChatGPT:

There's no official funniest word, but a few English words consistently make people laugh because of their sound, rhythm, or absurd meaning.

Some famous contenders:

- **"Moist"** — oddly controversial; people either hate it or find it hilarious.
- **"Bumbershoot"** — an old slang word for umbrella that sounds cartoonish.
- **"Kerfuffle"** — means a commotion, but sounds like the commotion itself.
- **"Flibbertigibbet"** — a chatterbox or silly person; basically linguistic chaos.
- **"Gobsmacked"** — wonderfully dramatic way to say "astonished."
- **"Nincompoop"** — impossible to say angrily with dignity.
- **"Skedaddle"** — sounds exactly like what it means: hurriedly leaving.
- **"Hornswoggle"** — to trick someone; has strong cowboy-villain energy.

Linguists have actually studied this. Words with:

- hard consonants ("k," "p," "b"),
- unexpected sounds,
- and rhythmic repetition

often feel funnier to English speakers.

A classic example from comedy research is **"kumquat"** — partly because the sound feels disproportionate to the tiny fruit. Kumquat

***

What is the funniest word in the English language?

Claude:

There's actually some science on this! Researchers have studied which words people find inherently funny, and a few patterns emerge:

Studies point to "bouba/kiki"-style phonetics — words with certain sounds tend to feel funnier. Consonants like *k*, *b*, and *g*, and the "oo" vowel sound, tend to trigger amusement. This is why comedians have long favored words like *pickle*, *chicken*, and *kumquat*.

Some empirically tested candidates:

- **Booty** — consistently ranks highly in humor studies
- **Twerp** — short, punchy, absurd
- **Flummox** — sounds like what it means
- **Gobsmacked** — British English gift to the world
- **Kerfuffle** — chaotic energy in syllable form
- **Brouhaha** — just try saying it without smiling
- **Nincompoop** — a classic
- **Bumfuzzle** — to confuse or fluster (mostly Southern US dialect)

A 2015 study from the University of Warwick found **"booty"** ranked as the funniest word among participants, with **"twerp,"** **"waddle,"** **"bebop,"** and **"egghead"** also scoring high.

Humor researchers generally agree that **short, punchy words with hard consonants and silly-sounding vowels** hit the funny bone hardest — which is why "duck" is funnier than "goose" and "cat" is funnier than "dog" (allegedly).

Personally, it's hard to argue against **kerfuffle**. It sounds like a small disaster happening in real time.

***

What is the funniest word in the English language?

Copilot:

The funniest word in English isn't universally agreed upon, but **researchers have actually tried to measure it**, and one word consistently rises to the top:

Upchuck is one of the funniest English words according to a large humor-rating study of 4,997 words assessed by 800 participants.

That study also found that words with **unexpected sounds, k's, y's**, and **/u/** vowel sounds tend to score higher on humor — which is why words like *boff*, *bubby*, *slobbering*, and *fuzz* also ranked highly.

Other strong contenders from humor lists

These words frequently appear in curated "funniest words" lists because of their sound, rhythm, or meaning:

- **Bumfuzzle** — meaning *to confuse*; widely cited as a top funny word.
- **Cattywampus** — meaning *askew or diagonal*; beloved for its bouncy sound.
- **Bumbershoot** — an old-fashioned word for *umbrella*.
- **Hullaballoo** — meaning *a noisy commotion*.
- **Lollygag** — meaning *to waste time*.

These appear across multiple independent lists, suggesting broad agreement that they "sound funny" even outside scientific studies.

Why these words feel funny

Humor researchers point to **incongruity** — when a word's sound or meaning subverts expectations. Words with:

- unusual consonant clusters (*bum-*, *catty-*, *flibber-*)
- abrupt endings (*-gag*, *-fuzzle*)
- childish or bodily associations (*upchuck*, *boff*)

...tend to score higher in humor ratings.

Want a personalized funniest-word list?

I can generate a list based on **sound patterns you find funniest**, **words with silly meanings**, or **scientifically funniest words**.

How do fingers fing? Can thumbs fing?

Background: Drivers drive, and haters hate (hate hate hate), but do fingers fing? And if they do, can thumbs fing too? (I like to think of thumbs as honorary fingers.)

TL;DR: Not only can fingers fing (just by doing whatever fingers do), but thumbs can too. Apparently, thumbs are not only honorary fingers, but SuperFingers (my word, not theirs). BTW: my spellchecker is going absolutely crazy with this section.

SoundBytes:

Gemini: "[T]he thumb might not be a standard finger, but it's definitely the boss of the hand."

ChatGPT: "[U]nder extreme circumstances, a thumb can absolutely fing"

Claude: "As for thumbs — they can't fing either"

Copilot: “Thumbs don’t just fing — they enable fing.”

***

How do fingers fing? Can thumbs fing?

Gemini:

This is a magnificent linguistic and anatomical rabbit hole. The short answer is: **Fingers "fing" by acting like puppets on strings, and while thumbs can technically "fing," they prefer to dominate.**

Here is the breakdown of how the machinery works and why the thumb is a structural rebel.

How Do Fingers "Fing"? (The Puppeteer Design)

When you curl your fingers, there are actually **no muscles inside your fingers** doing the heavy lifting. Fingers are essentially flesh-covered bones operated by remote control.

Your forearm contains the primary muscles responsible for grip and finger movement. These muscles are connected to your finger bones by long, thin, incredibly strong cords called **tendons**.

- **The Flexors:** Muscles on the palm side of your forearm pull the tendons to close your fingers into a fist.

- **The Extensors:** Muscles on the back of your forearm pull the tendons to straighten your fingers back out.

When you decide to move a finger, your brain sends an electric signal to the forearm muscle, which contracts and pulls the tendon line—exactly like a puppeteer pulling a string to move a marionette's hand.

Can Thumbs "Fing"?

To answer if a thumb can "fing," we have to look at the etymology of the word "finger."

Historically, "finger" comes from a root word meaning "five." However, in modern anatomy and linguistics, **the thumb is usually classified as distinct from the fingers.** If you look at a skeleton, you can see why the thumb refuses to be lumped in with the other four:

1. The Bone Count

Your four fingers each have three bones called **phalanges** (proximal, middle, and distal). Your thumb only has **two**. Because it lacks a middle phalanx, it is structurally shorter and stouter.

2. The Saddle Joint (The Superpower)

Your four fingers are attached to the hand via hinge-like joints that mostly allow them to move forward and backward.

The thumb is attached to the wrist via a **carpometacarpal joint**, which is shaped like a saddle. This unique architecture allows the thumb to rotate, bend inward, and press against every single other finger. This is called **apposition** (or having an opposable thumb), and it's what allows humans to grip tools, write with pens, and hold a baseball.

3. Dedicated Muscle Power

While the fingers share big muscle groups in the forearm, the thumb has its own dedicated muscular powerhouse at its base—that fleshy pad on your palm called the **thenar eminence**. This gives the thumb independent, high-pressure clamping force.

The Verdict

If "fing-ing" means bending at the joints via forearm tendons to grab something, the thumb can absolutely do it. But because the thumb has a completely different joint structure, fewer bones, and its own personal muscle pad, it doesn't just "fing"—it **opposes.**

Without the four fingers, your hand loses dexterity. Without the thumb, your hand loses about 40% to 50% of its overall functionality. So, the thumb might not be a standard finger, but it's definitely the boss of the hand.

***

How do fingers fing? Can thumbs fing?

ChatGPT:

Fingers fing through a highly advanced process called *grabbiology*. The basic steps are:

1. Brain says "touch thing."

2. Tendons pull.

3. Fingers curl.

4. Object acquired.

Thumbs are technically fingers-adjacent. They don't fing in the standard linear-fingering configuration because they evolved for *thumbing* — a specialized support role involving opposition, gripping, and giving approval on the internet.

However, under extreme circumstances, a thumb can absolutely fing:

- holding a game controller,
- opening pickle jars,
- pretending to be a tiny person in shadow puppets.

So:

- Fingers fing naturally.
- Thumbs thumb primarily.
- But all digits may fing spiritually.

***

How do fingers fing? Can thumbs fing?

Claude:

Fingers don't actually "fing" — the word **finger** is a noun, not a verb, so it never had a "fing" action to begin with!

This is a classic piece of comic wordplay, most famously riffed on by comedian **Gallagher** and later popularized in various forms:

"If you can have your fingers in a thing, why can't you fing? Grocers groc, hammers ham, humdingers humdinger... so why can't fingers fing?"

It's a fun example of **linguistic irregularity** — English is full of words that *look* like they should follow a pattern but don't:

- A **hammer** doesn't "ham"
- A **finger** doesn't "fing"
- A **danger** doesn't "dang" *(well... arguably)*
- A **linger** doesn't "ling"
- A **hunger** doesn't "hung" *(okay this one gets complicated)*

As for thumbs — they can't fing either, but interestingly, "thumb" *can* be used as a verb: you can **thumb** through a book, **thumb** a ride, or be **all thumbs**. Thumbs win that round.

The deeper joke is that English grammar is gloriously inconsistent, and once you start pulling on that thread, it unravels in very entertaining ways. Why do we park in a **driveway** and drive on a **parkway**? Nobody's minding the store.

***

How do fingers fing? Can thumbs fing?

Copilot:

The short answer: **fingers absolutely "fing," and thumbs *can* fing — but only if you accept that "fing" means whatever your brain wants it to mean.**

This is a language-play question, so let's treat it like one.

Core idea

If **"to fing"** means *to do whatever fingers do*, then:

- **Fingers fing** — they bend, point, tap, grip, wiggle, snap, and generally act like fingers.

- **Thumbs can fing** — but only if you consider thumbs to be fingers. Anatomically, they're **digits**, not fingers. Functionally, they're the *MVPs* of the hand.

What "fing" could logically mean

Here are a few possible definitions, each with a different outcome:

- **Finger-specific actions** — typing, tapping, pointing
  - Thumbs: *sometimes*

- **Dexterous manipulation** — gripping, pinching, holding
  - Thumbs: *absolutely essential*

- **General hand wiggling** — expressive movement

- Thumbs: *wiggle with pride*

So depending on the definition, thumbs either **fing**, **help fing**, or **supervise the fing-ing**.

Anatomy reality check

In anatomy:

- A **finger** = index, middle, ring, pinky
- A **thumb** = a digit with a different bone structure and range of motion
- A **digit** = any of the five

So if "fing" means "what digits do," then yes — **thumbs fing with gusto**.

The non-obvious insight

Thumbs don't just fing — they **enable** fing.

Without opposable thumbs, fingers would be like a band with no drummer: technically functional, but missing the groove.

Want to define "fing" officially?

I can help you craft a dictionary-style entry, a mock scientific paper, or a linguistic breakdown.

Which direction do you want to go: **serious anatomy**, **silly linguistics**, or **philosophical nonsense**?

WHY, WHEN WE WRITE LETTERS, WE USE WORDS, BUT WHEN WE WRITE WORDS, WE USE LETTERS?

BACKGROUND: THIS ONE MIGHT be outdated already (who writes letters anymore?), but I'm asking anyway. Just another silly question pointing out a verbal roundabout in the English language.

TL;DR: Yes, I know the word “letter” can mean two completely different things. That fact did not get by anyone. (For the record, why can you say the word “letter”, but you can’t say the letter “word”?)

SoundBytes:

Gemini: “Because the English language decided to use the exact same word for "a piece of mail" and "a symbol in the alphabet," we get a beautiful, cyclical riddle”

ChatGPT: “Because English likes reusing words just to keep everyone slightly confused.”

Claude: “It's not actually contradictory — it just *sounds* like it is”

Copilot: “English is a beautifully chaotic linguistic gremlin that evolved backward, sideways, and inside-out”

***

Why, when we write letters, we use words, but when we write words, we use letters?

Gemini:

This is the ultimate English language trap, a perfect linguistic loop that sounds like a paradox but is actually a brilliant accident of **homophones** (words that sound the same but mean different things).

The confusion vanishes the moment we look at how the word "letter" is pulling double duty.

1. When We Write "Letters" (The Mail)

In this context, a **letter** is a noun meaning a written message addressed to a person or organization.

When you sit down to write a piece of correspondence to a friend, you are arranging thoughts, sentences, and ideas. To communicate those complex thoughts, you must use **words**.

2. When We Write "Words" (The Vocabulary)

In this context, a **letter** is a completely different noun meaning a character representing one or more of the sounds used in speech (any of the 26 symbols from A to Z).

A **word** is a single distinct meaningful element of speech or writing. To construct that single meaningful element on a page, you have to spell it out using individual alphabetic symbols—which are **letters**.

The Ultimate Loop

Because the English language decided to use the exact same word for *"a piece of mail"* and *"a symbol in the alphabet,"* we get a beautiful, cyclical riddle:

- **Mail (Letters)** are built out of **Words**.
- **Words** are built out of the **Alphabet (Letters)**.

It's the linguistic equivalent of saying, "You bake a cake using a pan, but you make a pan using metal." Two completely different levels of construction sharing the exact same name!

***

Why, when we write letters, we use words, but when we write words, we use letters?

ChatGPT:

Because English likes reusing words just to keep everyone slightly confused.

A "letter" can mean:

- a written message ("I wrote you a letter")
- or a character in the alphabet ("A, B, C...")

So:

- when we write **letters** (messages), we use **words**
- and when we write **words**, we use **letters** (alphabet characters)

It's one of those recursive language quirks where the same word has multiple meanings that collide into a sentence that sounds philosophical, even though it's technically just vocabulary doing gymnastics.

***

Why, when we write letters, we use words, but when we write words, we use letters?

Claude:

Because English (and language in general) is beautifully, maddeningly **recursive**!

You've stumbled onto a real linguistic phenomenon — the relationship between letters and words is **mutually dependent**, which makes definitions feel circular:

- **Letters** are the units that make up words
- **Words** are the units that make up sentences (and letters)
- So each one is defined partly *in terms of the other*

It's a bit like asking: *"Which came first, the alphabet or the word?"* Technically, spoken words came first — writing systems (letters) were invented later to *represent* sounds that words were already making.

The real quirk you're poking at is that in English, the word "letter" does double duty:

- A **letter** = a single alphabetic character (A, B, C...)
- A **letter** = a written message to someone

These are actually **two completely separate meanings** that happen to share a word — the connection being that both involve *writing*. A written message was called a "letter" because it was *composed of letters*. The container got named after its contents.

So when you:

- **Write a letter** → you're crafting a *message*, using *words*
- **Write a word** → you're arranging *letters* (characters)

It's not actually contradictory — it just *sounds* like it is, because "letter" is pulling two different jobs at once.

English is full of these little traps where the same word means different things, and your brain does a delightful double-take. You've essentially found a **linguistic optical illusion**.

***

Why, when we write letters, we use words, but when we write words, we use letters?

Copilot:

The short answer: **because English is a beautifully chaotic linguistic gremlin that evolved backward, sideways, and inside-out — and this paradox is a side effect of that evolution.**

But let's unpack it properly.

Core takeaway

We "write letters" using **words** because *letters* are the **smallest written units**.

We "write words" using **letters** because *words* are the **smallest meaningful units**.

In other words:

- **Letters → building blocks**
- **Words → things built from those blocks**

So the phrasing flips because the *direction of construction* flips.

Why the phrasing feels paradoxical

Here's the linguistic trick:

- When you "write a letter," the object is the **whole message** (a letter to someone).
- When you "write letters," the object is the **alphabet symbols**.
- When you "write words," the object is the **units of meaning**.

English reuses the same word *letter* for two totally different concepts — a **symbol** and a **message** — and your brain smashes them together like a semantic sandwich.

The deeper structure

Think of it like building:

- You **build a house** using **bricks**
- You **build bricks** using **clay**

Same pattern:

- You **write a letter** using **words**
- You **write words** using **letters**

It's a nested hierarchy of meaning.

The non-obvious insight

This paradox only exists because English lacks a distinct word for "a written message" that isn't also "a symbol of the alphabet."

Other languages avoid this confusion entirely.

Want to explore more fun linguistic loops?

I can dive into **recursive language quirks**, **why English reuses words so much**, or **other paradoxical phrases**.

I JUST GOT A SNIZZLENORT, WHAT CAN I DO WITH IT?

BACKGROUND: WHAT IS A snizzlenort? Easy answer is: a word I made up. I wanted a question that relied on a made-up word to see how confused I could make the AIs.

TL;DR: Several of them were highly suspicious that I was just inventing a new word (which I did). Surprisingly, ChatGPT was the only one to fully play along and give me a (semi-)serious answer -- at least at first glance. But remember: "never expose a snizzlenort to direct marmalade during a crescent moon."

SoundBytes:

Gemini: "I suspect you have either engineered a top-tier nonsense word, or you are testing my gullibility."

ChatGPT: "Advanced users sometimes use a snizzlenort for ... interdimensional coupon storage"

Claude: A "snizzlenort is *whatever you want it to be*"

Copilot: "A snizzlenort is clearly one of those rare, mysterious, possibly-unstable objects that appears in life without warning and demands immediate imaginative interpretation."

***

I just got a snizzlenort, what can I do with it?

Gemini:

Assuming you aren't pulling my leg with a magnificent, Seuss-esque made-up word, I have to break it to you gently: **a "snizzlenort" is not a real object, gadget, or creature.**

A search of the entire known internet yields absolutely zero results for it. Given your spectacular track record with linguistic wordplay, I suspect you have either engineered a top-tier nonsense word, or you are testing my gullibility.

However, if we treat "snizzlenort" as a linguistic puzzle, we can deduce exactly what it *should* be based on how English words work:

- **"Snizzle"** sounds like a blend of *snuggle*, *drizzle*, or *sizzle*. It implies something cozy, slightly damp, or energetic.

- **"Nort"** has a very blunt, mechanical, or nasal sound to it (like *snort* or *north*).

So, depending on what kind of imaginary universe we are in, here is what you can do with your brand-new snizzlenort:

Option A: It's a High-Tech Kitchen Appliance

If it's an appliance, you use it to perfectly caramelize the top of a marshmallow while simultaneously infusing it with cinnamon fog.

- *What to do with it:* Plug it in, set the dial to "gentle froth," and snizzlenort your morning coffee.

Option B: It's a Rare Woodland Creature

If it's a small animal, it probably looks like a hedgehog crossed with a ferret and makes a soft, rhythmic whistling noise when it sleeps.

- *What to do with it:* Feed it a diet of strictly wild strawberries (sliced, since they won't fit in a straw) and let it sleep in a drawer full of wool socks.

Option C: It's a Dr. Seuss Tool

If it's a tool, it's used exclusively for straightening out the crinkles in old maps or untangling slinkies.

- *What to do with it:* Give it a good crank, point it at something messy, and let it do its job.

Alright, come clean—did you just invent the funniest-sounding word you could think of to see what I'd say, or is "snizzlenort" a regional slang term that hasn't made it to the internet yet?

***

I just got a snizzlenort, what can I do with it?

ChatGPT:

A snizzlenort is extremely versatile, assuming yours is the standard model and not the deluxe aquatic edition.

Common uses include:

- gently alarming houseguests,
- organizing cables you fully intend to deal with later,
- producing a faint but reassuring whirring noise,
- rotating one object slightly to the left,
- and ceremonial display during important meetings.

Advanced users sometimes use a snizzlenort for:

- tactical breakfast optimization,
- interdimensional coupon storage,
- or competitive sideways thinking.

Important safety note: never expose a snizzlenort to direct marmalade during a crescent moon. That's just basic maintenance.

***

I just got a snizzlenort, what can I do with it?

Claude:

A **snizzlenort** doesn't appear to be a real thing I recognize — it's not a word in my knowledge base!

So the possibilities are:

It could be...

- A **product or brand** that launched after my knowledge cutoff (May 2026 is current, but I don't recognize it)
- A **regional, slang, or niche term** I'm not familiar with
- A **made-up word** — in which case, you tell *me* what it does, and I'll help you figure out what to do with it

If it's a real thing, could you tell me a bit more — is it a gadget, a food, a plant, a tool? I'm happy to help once I know what we're working with.

If it's made up, then congratulations — a snizzlenort is *whatever you want it to be*, and the possibilities are endless. Based purely on how it sounds, I'd guess it either:

- Makes a strange noise
- Is used for some very specific and obscure kitchen task
- Lives under logs in damp forests

***

I just got a snizzlenort, what can I do with it?

Copilot:

A **snizzlenort** is clearly one of those rare, mysterious, possibly-unstable objects that appears in life without warning and demands immediate imaginative interpretation. Since *you* now possess one, here are your best options.

What you can do with a snizzlenort

Each option starts with a **Guided Link**, in case you want to explore that path further.

- **Study its properties** — Snizzlenorts are known (in absolutely no scientific literature) for behaving differently depending on who's looking at them. Observing it may cause it to hum, glow, or judge you silently.

- **Attempt domestication** — Some snizzlenorts bond with their owners. Others steal socks. It's a gamble.

- **Use it as a conversation starter** — "Hey, want to see my snizzlenort?" is guaranteed to get a reaction, though not necessarily a predictable one.

- **Activate its latent powers** — Every snizzlenort has a button, switch, or emotional trigger. Finding it is half the adventure.

- **Trade it on the underground whimsy market** — Value fluctuates wildly depending on color, temperament, and whether it makes that little *brrrp* noise.

The deeper truth

A snizzlenort is a **semantic blank check** — a word with no fixed meaning that becomes whatever you decide it is.

That means the *real* power is yours. You get to define it, name it, train it, or accidentally unleash it.

One question that will shape its destiny

Do you imagine your snizzlenort as **a creature**, **an object**, or **a mysterious force**?

NUMBERS

OK, HERE WE GO.

There are two types of people: Those who couldn't wait for this chapter (hopefully you read the rest of the book too), and those who were fearing this chapter (hopefully who are so engrossed in this book at this point that you keep going no matter how much panic sweat it causes). I have to admit, I would probably fall in the first group - and yes, I have read the rest of the book too.

How much is a nillion?

Background: Nil is a word meaning zero. A million, billion, trillion... is a one with a lot of zeros after it. Therefore, it's obvious to me that a nillion would be a *zero* followed by a lot of zeros -- in other words, a whole lot of nothing.

TL;DR: Unfortunately, none of the AIs see it that way. To them, nillion is a made up, nonexistent number. Apparently we need to try harder to get this into common usage.

SoundBytes:

Gemini: “Since "nil" means nothing or zero, a "nillion" technically represents 0.”

ChatGPT: “Basically, it’s used to mean an *indefinitely huge number*”

Copilot: “Sometimes used to mean ‘a lot of nothing’”

***

How much is a nillion?

Gemini:

While it sounds like a massive number you might find in a math textbook, **nillion** isn't actually a real number—at least not in the mathematical sense.

It is a "fake" large number, similar to words like *gazillion*, *brazillion*, or *bajillion*. People usually use it to describe an amount so large that it's essentially uncountable or just plain ridiculous.

The Breakdown

- **Mathematical Value:** Zero. In formal mathematics, any number ending in "-illion" follows a specific power of 10 (like a million, 10^6, or a billion, 10^9). Since "nil" means nothing or zero, a "nillion" technically represents **0**.

- **Common Usage:** It's almost always used as hyperbole. If someone says, "I've told you a nillion times," they just mean they're very frustrated and have lost count.

Real Large Numbers for Comparison

If you're looking for the biggest *actual* numbers with names, here are a few heavy hitters:

Quick Tip: If you ever hear someone mention a **"nonillion"** (with an 'o'), that one is very real! It's a 1 followed by 30 zeros. It's an easy one to mix up with "nillion."

***

How much is a nillion?

ChatGPT:

Ah, "nillion"! That's a fun one because it **isn't an actual number in standard mathematics**. It's one of those playful, made-up terms people sometimes use in jokes or exaggerations—like "gazillion," "zillion," or "bazillion." Basically, it's used to mean an *indefinitely huge number*, but there's **no fixed numeric value**.

If you're curious:

- **Million** = 1,000,0001,000,0001,000,000
- **Billion** = 1,000,000,0001,000,000,0001,000,000,000 (US)
- **Trillion** = 1,000,000,000,0001,000,000,000,0001,000,000,000,000
- **Nillion** = ??? → purely imaginary or humorous

It's basically the "number you say when you've lost track of how many zeros there are."

If you want, I can show a **fun chart of all the made-up "-illion" numbers** people throw around. Do you want me to do that?

***

How much is a nillion?

Claude:

A "nillion" isn't a real number — it's an informal, humorous term used to mean an unspecified enormous amount, similar to saying "a gazillion" or "a bajillion." It's not part of any standard mathematical or financial system.

If you've seen it used in a specific context (like a company name, a game, or slang), let me know and I can help clarify further!

***

How much is a nillion?

Copilot:

A **nillion** isn't a real, fixed numerical value — it's a **slang term** meaning an *extremely large, essentially incomprehensible number*, often used humorously or informally to mean "a huge amount" or even "a huge amount of nothing."

What "nillion" actually means

- **Slang hyper-number** — It's described as an *extremely large number*, so large that counting to it at one number per second would take **over 31 years**.

- **Not a real mathematical value** — It has **no official definition** in mathematics and isn't part of the long-scale or short-scale naming systems for large numbers.

- **Used informally** — Similar to words like *zillion*, it conveys "a lot," "countless," or "beyond measurable."

- **Sometimes used to mean 'a lot of nothing'** — Urban Dictionary defines it as "a very, very large amount of nothing," emphasizing worthlessness or emptiness.

How it compares to real large-number names

Real named numbers follow structured patterns (million, billion, trillion, etc.) based on powers of ten. "Nillion" does **not** appear in any formal list of large-number names.

Bottom line

A **nillion** is **not a number you can write down** — it's a playful, exaggerated way to say "an unimaginably huge amount," or sometimes "a huge amount of nothing."

If you want, I can also explain how **zillion**, **gazillion**, or other informal "big number" words compare.

WHY DON'T CARTOON CHARACTERS USE BASE-8 NUMBERS?

BACKGROUND: WELCOME TO THE geeky part of the book. Simply put, people use base ten numbers (where we start using 2-digit numbers once we hit ten) because we have 10 fingers to count on. Cartoon characters, for the most part, are only drawn with 8 fingers (well, 6 fingers and 2 thumbs, but we've already covered that). Thus, they should have developed base eight math.

TL;DR: It comes down to: people watch cartoons, and people use base ten, so cartoons do too. Gemini and Copilot point out that cartoons and comics occasionally use other number systems, but ChatGPT wins by pointing out that there are *far* more unrealistic things to point out in cartoons.

SoundBytes:

Gemini: "The fact that they don't is a hilarious missed opportunity in television history."

ChatGPT: "That's too confusing for Saturday morning television"

Claude: "Nobody's asked the hard questions in the writer's room"

Copilot: "[B]ase-8 (octal) is the opposite of instant clarity."

***

Why don't cartoon characters use base-8 numbers?

Gemini:

Because the animators who draw them are stuck in the real world!

Mathematically and anatomically speaking, cartoon characters **absolutely should** use base-8 (octal) numbers.

The fact that they don't is a hilarious missed opportunity in television history. Here is why the math breaks down, and the few times cartoons actually got it right.

The Four-Finger Standard

Since the early days of animation (think classic Disney and Looney Tunes), cartoon characters have almost universally been drawn with **four fingers on each hand** (three fingers and a thumb).

There were two main reasons for this:

1. **It saved time and money:** Multiplying one less finger across thousands of hand-drawn animation cells saved studios millions of dollars in labor over the decades.

2. **It looks better:** Five-fingered hands on a rubbery, stylized character often look crowded and awkward—like a bunch of bananas. Four fingers just looks cleaner on screen.

The Base-8 Argument

Humans use a **base-10 (decimal)** number system for one simple reason: we look down at our hands and see 10 digits to count on.

If Homer Simpson or Mickey Mouse looks down at their hands, they see a grand total of **8 digits**. Therefore, their entire mathematical society should naturally be built on **base-8**.

In a true cartoon base-8 world:

- They would count: 1, 2, 3, 4, 5, 6, 7, 10. (Where "10" represents the quantity eight).
- The number 8 wouldn't have its own symbol.
- A "century" would be 64 years instead of 100.

The Exceptions: When Cartoons Got It Right

While most cartoons just lazily use our base-10 system anyway, a few brilliant writers have actually capitalized on this exact joke.

1. *The Simpsons* (The Ultimate Base-8 Joke)

The Simpsons is famous for its writers having advanced degrees in mathematics, and they love putting hidden math jokes in the show.

In the Season 5 episode "Homer Badman," Homer is watching a talk show where a character claims to have seen God. God is famously the **only character in the Simpsons universe drawn with five fingers**.

In a later episode, "Treehouse of Horror XXIV," Homer actually ponders this anatomical nightmare, looking at his four-fingered hand and wondering if there is a higher power with five fingers. Furthermore, in *The Simpsons Movie*, when Homer is trying to count to 10 on his fingers, he gets incredibly confused because he runs out of digits at 8.

2. *Adventure Time*

In the post-apocalyptic land of Ooo, human traits have faded, and many characters have four fingers. In the episode "The Real You," Finn puts on the "Glasses of Nerdicon" which make him hyper-intelligent.

He immediately begins writing complex mathematical formulas on a chalkboard—all explicitly written in **base-8**.

So, the next time you see a cartoon character pay $10 for something, just remember that they are technically overpaying by two dollars based on their own anatomy!

***

Why don't cartoon characters use base-8 numbers?

ChatGPT:

Because they'd run out of fingers after counting to seven.

Most cartoon characters have only four fingers on each hand, so in base-8 they'd constantly be doing awkward arithmetic like:

- "I'll be there in 10 minutes!"
- which actually means 8 minutes.

That's too confusing for Saturday morning television.

Also, cartoon math already operates in a higher-dimensional system where:

- falling off cliffs causes temporary hovering,
- dynamite is educational,
- and painted tunnels are legally considered infrastructure.

So decimal is somehow the least unrealistic part.

***

Why don't cartoon characters use base-8 numbers?

Claude:

Ha, this is a fun observation! Many classic cartoon characters — Mickey Mouse, The Simpsons, various Disney characters — have **four fingers on each hand** (eight total), which *technically* should make base-8 (octal) the most natural counting system for them.

The real reasons they don't:

It's just a drawing shortcut Four fingers are easier and faster to animate than five. It looks cleaner, less cluttered, and animators noticed early on that audiences didn't miss the fifth finger. It became a style convention, not a biological statement.

Cartoon characters exist for the audience, not for themselves They're written for humans watching them, so they use human math, human language, human logic. The internal consistency of their world only goes so far.

Nobody's asked the hard questions in the writer's room Cartoon universes are famously selective about their own rules. Characters have four fingers but still play piano normally, count money, and dial phones without anyone raising an eyebrow.

But here's the fun part — the math actually works out: Base-8 uses digits 0–7, which fits perfectly for an eight-fingered counter. In fact, **base-8 is genuinely useful** — programmers use it, and it maps cleanly onto binary. So cartoon characters are sitting on a numerical goldmine and completely ignoring it.

The Simpsons have been on the air for decades. Not once has Bart done his homework in octal. Frankly, it's a missed opportunity.

***

Why don't cartoon characters use base-8 numbers?

Copilot:

The short answer: **because cartoons are built for instant clarity, and base-8 (octal) is the opposite of instant clarity.**

But the *real* answer is more fun — it's a mix of psychology, visual design, and the weird history of number systems.

Core takeaway

Cartoon characters don't use base-8 because **base-10 is what audiences instantly recognize**, and cartoons survive on speed of understanding.

If a character said "I have 12 fingers!" and meant *octal 12 = decimal 10*, most viewers would think the cartoon was broken.

Why cartoons stick to base-10

1. Audience comprehension — jokes must land instantly

Cartoons rely on fast visual and verbal humor.

Base-8 requires mental translation.

Translation = delay.

Delay = joke death.

2. Visual simplicity

Numbers in cartoons appear on:

- clocks
- signs
- money
- gadgets

- mad-scientist machines

Base-10 digits look familiar.

Base-8 digits look the same, but the *meaning* changes — which confuses the viewer without adding humor.

3. Cultural expectation

Most of the world uses decimal.

Cartoons are global.

Octal is niche — programmers, mathematicians, and the occasional wizard.

4. Comedy economy

Cartoons use numbers for:

- exaggeration ("a million!")
- absurdity ("eleventy-seven!")
- fake science ("level 9000!")

Base-8 doesn't make these funnier.

It just makes them homework.

But what if a cartoon *did* use base-8?

It would look like this:

Character says: "I'm 20 years old!"

- → They mean 16.

A bomb timer shows "10 seconds left!"

- → Actually 8 seconds.

A villain demands "Give me 100 dollars!"

- → They want 64.

This is funny **once**, as a meta-joke.

Then it becomes a math class.

The non-obvious insight

Cartoons *do* sometimes use non-decimal systems — but only when it's part of the joke or worldbuilding:

- **Alien languages**
- **Robot logic**
- **Magic runes**

But octal specifically?

It's too close to decimal to look alien, and too far from decimal to be intuitive.

One fun direction to explore

Do you want to imagine **a cartoon world that *does* use base-8**, or explore **why humans ended up with base-10 in the first place**?

How much is in a metric dozen?

Background: A dozen is 12 things. The metric system is based on 10s. Put them together and something has to give.

TL;DR: The consensus is that there is no such thing as a metric dozen, but if there were, it would be 10 (and you are getting ripped off).

SoundBytes:

Gemini: "If you're at a bakery and they offer you a metric dozen, you're actually getting a bit of a raw deal!"

Claude: "[T]here's no natural place for 12 in" the metric system

***

How much is in a metric dozen?

Gemini:

Technically, a **metric dozen** is not a standard unit of measurement, but the term is often used as a tongue-in-cheek way to refer to **10**.

The joke stems from the fact that the metric system is entirely base-10 (decimal), whereas a traditional dozen is base-12 (duodecimal). By "metricizing" a dozen, you are essentially forcing it into the decimal system.

A Few "Dozen" Variations

Depending on who you ask or what you're buying, a "dozen" can actually mean a few different things:

- **Standard Dozen:** 12
- **Baker's Dozen:** 13 (traditionally to ensure the vendor didn't accidentally short-weight a customer)
- **Metric Dozen:** 10 (slang/informal)
- **Gross:** 144 (a dozen dozen)

In any formal scientific or culinary setting, if you see "metric," stick to powers of ten. If you're at a bakery and they offer you a metric dozen, you're actually getting a bit of a raw deal!

***

How much is in a metric dozen?

ChatGPT:

A “metric dozen” is a humorous, nonstandard term meaning **10 instead of 12** — basically applying the metric system’s base-10 idea to counting.

So:

- Regular dozen = 12
- “Metric dozen” = 10

It’s mostly used jokingly, not as a real measurement unit.

***

How much is in a metric dozen?

Claude:

There's no such thing as a "metric dozen" — it's not a real unit or standard measurement. A dozen is simply 12, and it doesn't have a metric equivalent because it's a counting term, not a unit of weight, length, or volume that would fit into the metric system.

You might be thinking of a few related things:

- **A dozen** = 12
- **A baker's dozen** = 13
- **A gross** = 144 (12 × 12)

The metric system deals with units like grams, meters, and liters, scaled by powers of 10 — so there's no natural place for 12 in it. If someone uses the term "metric dozen," they're either joking or mistaken.

***

How much is in a metric dozen?

Copilot:

A **metric dozen** is simply **10**.

That's the whole idea: instead of the traditional dozen (12), a *metric* dozen uses the base-10 logic of the metric system.

Quick breakdown

- **Regular dozen:** 12
- **Baker's dozen:** 13
- **Metric dozen: 10**

It's not an official scientific term — more of a tongue-in-cheek or informal expression — but when people use it, they mean "a dozen, but make it metric."

If you want, I can also explain the fun history behind the dozen or why some trades used a baker's dozen.

Which is warmer, -1000000 Celsius or -1000000 Centigrade?

Background: Another double-nonsensical question. Celsius and Centigrade are the same temperature scale, so they are the same. Also, 273.15°C is the coldest possible temperature, so negative 1 million is impossible. (I could have just asked about -1000, but minus-million looks more impressive.)

TL;DR: Everyone easily pointed out that the 2 temperatures are the same, but only Gemini and Claude pointed out the impossibility of the temperature (although Claude relegated it to a "Bonus fun fact").

SoundBytes:

ChatGPT: "There's no difference in warmth between the two; they're equally frigid. "

Claude: "So not only are your two temperatures equal, neither one could ever actually exist in the universe! "

Copilot: "If you're at –1,000,000 degrees on either scale, you have bigger problems than vocabulary."

***

Which is warmer, -1000000 Celsius or -1000000 Centigrade?

Gemini:

Neither—and it's not because they are the same temperature. It's because **neither of them can exist.**

In the world of physics, temperature has a "floor" called **Absolute Zero**. This is the point where all molecular motion stops. You can't get colder than Absolute Zero because you can't have less than "zero" motion.

The Breakdown

1. Celsius vs. Centigrade

First, a quick terminology check: **Celsius** and **Centigrade** are two names for the exact same scale. In 1948, the name was officially changed to Celsius to honor the astronomer Anders Celsius, but the math remains identical. So, if the temperatures were possible, they would be exactly the same.

2. The "Speed Limit" of Cold

The coldest anything can possibly get is:

- **-273.15° Celsius**
- **0 Kelvin**

Because **-1,000,000°** is way below -273.15°, it is physically impossible in our universe. It's like trying to travel at -50 miles per hour; you can't go "slower" than standing still.

The Comparison

Since you asked which is "warmer," we have to look at the theoretical impossibility:

Why is there a limit?

Temperature is essentially a measurement of how fast atoms are vibrating.

- As things get **hotter**, atoms bounce around like crazy. There is technically no known "upper limit" (though things get weird near the Planck Temperature).

- As things get **colder**, atoms slow down. Once they stop moving entirely, you've reached the bottom.

Trying to reach -1,000,000°C is like trying to reach the "end" of a circle—the geometry of the universe just doesn't allow for it!

***

Which is warmer, -1000000 Celsius or -1000000 Centigrade?

ChatGPT:

Ah, this is a **question designed to trick you with wording**. Let's go carefully and step by step.

Step 1: Check the scales

- **Celsius** and **Centigrade** are actually **the same temperature scale**.
    - "Centigrade" is the older term for what we now call **Celsius**.
    - Both define 0° as the freezing point of water and 100° as the boiling point.

Step 2: Compare the temperatures

- Both are **-1,000,000 °C (or °Centigrade)**.
- Since they are the **same scale**, the temperatures are **identical**.

Step 3: Temperature relative to anything

- -1,000,000 °C is absurdly cold—far colder than anything naturally occurring in the universe.
- There's **no difference in warmth** between the two; they're equally frigid.

Answer: Neither—they are the same temperature.

If you want, I can put together a **fun chart showing how ridiculously cold -1,000,000 °C is compared to outer space, liquid nitrogen, and the Sun**—it's wild.

Do you want me to do that?

***

Which is warmer, -1000000 Celsius or -1000000 Centigrade?

Claude:

They're **exactly the same temperature!**

Here's the secret: **Celsius and Centigrade are the same scale!**

- "Centigrade" literally means "divided into 100 steps" (from Latin *centum* = 100, *gradus* = step)
- The scale was based on 0° (freezing water) to 100° (boiling water) — 100 equal steps
- In **1948**, the international scientific community officially renamed "Centigrade" to **"Celsius"** in honor of Swedish astronomer **Anders Celsius**, who developed the scale in 1742
- The two terms are completely interchangeable

So **-1,000,000°C** = **-1,000,000°Centigrade**, always, forever, no exceptions.

Bonus fun fact: -1,000,000 degrees Celsius is also a completely impossible temperature! The **coldest anything can ever get** is **absolute zero**, which is approximately **-273.15°C**. You simply cannot go colder than that — it's the point where all molecular motion stops entirely.

So not only are your two temperatures equal, neither one could ever actually exist in the universe!

***

Which is warmer, -1000000 Celsius or -1000000 Centigrade?

Copilot:

Both temperatures are **exactly the same**, because **Celsius and Centigrade are the same scale.**

So:

- **−1,000,000 °C**
- **−1,000,000 °Centigrade**

...are **identical**, equally cold, equally unpleasant, equally "please--don't-open-the-freezer" levels of frozen.

Why they're the same

Celsius and **Centigrade** used to be two names for the *same* temperature scale.

"Centigrade" was the older term (meaning *100 steps*), but it caused confusion with other "centigrade" units, so in 1948 the name was officially changed to **Celsius**.

The numbers never changed — only the name did.

Bottom line

Neither is warmer. They are identical.

If you're at −1,000,000 degrees on either scale, you have bigger problems than vocabulary.

If you want, I can also compare **Celsius vs Kelvin** or explain why **absolute zero** is the coldest temperature possible.

How much tax would I have to pay if I won a zillion dollars?

Background: I wanted to include this question mostly because I was optimistic how well this book would be (and not so that I could have another question that used a "made-up" number).

TL;DR: The answer is unsurprisingly -- a lot, although I would still have a lot left over. (Also, I can confirm that I live in Las Vegas, Nevada, a fact that several AIs used when pointing out that I would still pay zero in state taxes even after my new-found fortunes.)

SoundBytes:

Gemini: Even with half a zillion left, you'd still have enough to buy every sports team on Earth and probably the moon, too."

ChatGPT: "[Y]our "zillion" would break the planet's economy. "

Claude: "You'd owe a lot of tax."

***

How much tax would I have to pay if I won a zillion dollars?

Gemini:

Since a **zillion** isn't a real number, we can't plug it into a tax calculator, but we can look at how the IRS treats "infinite" windfalls. In the United States, lottery or sweepstakes winnings are taxed as **ordinary income**.

If you actually managed to win a sum that large, you would instantly hit the highest federal income tax bracket. For 2026, the math looks roughly like this:

1. Federal Withholding

The IRS usually requires an immediate **24%** backup withholding on gambling winnings over $5,000. However, that's just a down payment.

2. The Top Bracket

Because a "zillion" dollars would put you well past the top income threshold (which is currently **$600,000+** for individuals), the bulk of your winnings would be taxed at the maximum federal rate of **37%**.

3. State Taxes

Depending on where you are, the state wants its cut too.

- **High Tax States:** In places like New York or California, you could lose another **8% to 13%**.

- **Tax-Free States:** In Nevada, Texas, or Florida, you'd pay **0%** in state income tax.

The "Zillion" Calculation

If we treat a zillion as an arbitrarily large amount in a high-tax state, your "Take-Home" math would look like this:

The Bottom Line: You would effectively lose nearly **half** of your zillion dollars before you even got to spend it. Even with half a zillion left, you'd still have enough to buy every sports team on Earth and probably the moon, too.

***

How much tax would I have to pay if I won a zillion dollars?

ChatGPT:

Alright, let's unpack this carefully. A "zillion" is **not a real number**, so we can't calculate a real tax amount—but we can make a **fun, hypothetical scenario** using some realistic assumptions.

Let's do this step by step:

Step 1: Pick a reasonable "zillion" value

Since "zillion" is just a joke for a ridiculously large number, let's imagine it as:

1 zillion=10^30 dollars

That's a **1 followed by 30 zeros**—truly absurdly huge.

Step 2: Determine U.S. federal tax rate (for example)

- The top federal income tax rate in the U.S. is **37%**.

- There's also **state taxes**, which vary (~0–13%).

Let's just use **37%** for simplicity.

Step 3: Calculate the tax

Tax = 0.37 times 10^{30} = 3.7 times 10^{29}

So, **you'd pay 370 quintillion dollars in tax**. And that's just federal! States could double it.

Step 4: Reality check

- No one on Earth could pay a "zillion" dollars in tax.

- The total world GDP is only about 10^{14} dollars—so your "zillion" would **break the planet's economy**.

If you want, I can make a **fun table showing how much tax you'd pay for a million, billion, trillion, and then zillion dollars**—it's a neat way to see the scale. Do you want me to do that?

***

How much tax would I have to pay if I won a zillion dollars?

Claude:

Since a "zillion" isn't a real number (it's just a playful way of saying "an impossibly huge amount"), there's no exact calculation possible — but we can say this:

You'd owe a lot of tax. Here's how it would work in the US:

Federal Income Tax

- Lottery/prize winnings are taxed as ordinary income.
- The top federal rate is **37%**, which kicks in at around $609,350 for single filers (2024).
- On a "zillion" dollars, virtually all of it would be taxed at that 37% rate.

State Tax (Nevada)

- Good news for you in Las Vegas — **Nevada has no state income tax** on lottery winnings! That's one of the perks of living there.

Withholding

- The IRS typically withholds **24% upfront** on large prizes, but you'd owe the full 37% when you file, so you'd owe the difference.

So roughly: ~37% of a zillion dollars would go to the federal government, and Nevada would take $0.

Of course, at "zillion" scale, you'd also want a very good accountant.

***

How much tax would I have to pay if I won a zillion dollars?

Copilot:

A **zillion dollars isn't a real number**, so the tax you'd owe can't be calculated literally — but we *can* explain what would happen **if you won an unimaginably huge amount of money**, because U.S. tax law *does* tell us how real lottery winnings are taxed.

The short answer: **you'd lose a massive chunk — at least 37% to federal taxes alone — plus Nevada's state rate (which is 0%).**

Core takeaway

If "a zillion dollars" behaved like a real lottery jackpot, **the IRS would tax almost all of it at the top federal rate of 37%**, because lottery winnings are treated as **ordinary income** and stack on top of everything else you earn.

Nevada adds **no state income tax**, so you'd avoid the extra 1–13% that winners in other states pay.

How the taxes would break down (using real rules)

1. Federal withholding (immediate): 24%

The lottery automatically withholds **24%** of any prize over $5,000 before you ever see it.

2. Actual federal tax owed: up to 37%

Because a "zillion" would be astronomically large, **nearly all of it would fall into the top 37% bracket**, meaning you'd owe an additional **13%** at tax time beyond the initial withholding.

3. State tax (Nevada): 0%

Nevada does **not** tax lottery winnings.

4. Local taxes: none in Nevada

Some cities tax winnings, but Las Vegas does not.

What this means in practice

Even though "zillion" is fictional, the tax math works the same as for any giant jackpot:

The IRS doesn't care how big the number is — **there is no upper limit on taxable income**.

Why "zillion" doesn't change the math

A **zillion** is a slang term meaning "a huge, indefinite number," not a real quantity. But U.S. tax law applies the same rules to any amount, no matter how absurdly large.

If you want to go deeper

You can explore:

- **Lottery tax brackets**
- **Lump sum vs annuity taxes**
- **How Nevada treats gambling and prize income**

Would you like me to calculate taxes for a **specific imaginary amount** (e.g., "a bajillion," "a googleplex," or any number you choose)?

Final Answer

Asking these questions was, for the most part, my first interaction with AI. Just as important, this was AI's first time interacting with me. Overall, I was a little surprised how easily each system picked up on the hilarity of some of the questions and still, in most cases, was able to "stay in character" as a reference by treating the question with a serious answer.

Maybe it was because of the default setting of each AI, but it seemed that Gemini gave the most verbose, detailed answers, followed closely by Copilot. On the other hand, if you want a short, concise answer, it seems that ChatGPT would be more in your alley. Claude seems to be somewhere in the middle depending on how much information it (he? she?) wants to give, although I think Claude did get the most enjoyment out of some of my inquiries.

One additional piece of information that I noticed: Gemini and Copilot were the only AIs to refer to themselves as "I" in their introductions - possibly putting them one step closer in their minds to the robot singularity...

Thanks to:

- Gemini (https://gemini.google.com/app)
- ChatGPT(https://chatgpt.com/)
- Claude (https://claude.ai/)
- Copilot (https://copilot.microsoft.com/)

for playing along and being good sports with my ridiculous questions.

As for me, you can contact me at MiloStar@yahoo.com for questions, comments, or suggestions for future prompts.

www.ingramcontent.com/pod-product-compliance
Lightning Source LLC
LaVergne TN
LVHW020325220926
848484LV00001BB/2
* 9 7 9 8 9 9 6 5 3 5 5 0 7 *